NOVELSMITHING

The Structural Foundation
of Plot, Character, and Narration

The Psychic Origins of Myth,
the Mythic Origins of Storytelling

by

David Sheppard

Published in the United States of America by
Tragedy's Workshop, Healdsburg, CA
ISBN-13: 978-0-9818007-1-4
ISBN-10: 0-9818007-1-8
Cover illustration and design by Richard Sheppard

Publisher Web Site:
www.tragedysworkshop.com

Book Web Site:
www.novelsmithing.com

FOR

All the unpublished
novelsmiths of the world.

Acknowledgements

First of all, I want to thank New Mexico State University – Carlsbad for supporting my classes on both novel writing and Greek mythology. This book is a direct result of those classes. A special thank you to Richard Sheppard for the cover illustration, layout and design, and internal graphics, and to Marilyn Mueller, my editor, for her hard work and expertise.

I also want to thank all those who visited an earlier version of these pages on the Internet (under the title *Jungian Novel Writing*), and particularly those who took the time to contact me by email. Their favorable responses gave me the incentive to publish it in paperback.

Contents

Preface

The ancient Greeks knew the blacksmith as the priest of metals and his smithy as a temple to the gods.[1] Fire also had a prominent place in the ancient religion:

> The role of fire in ancient Greek religion is all-pervasive: whether in the sacrificial flame burning on the god's altar, the funeral pyre in human burial, or the torch-light which characterized nocturnal festivals and, in particular, mystery cults. … It remained always a medium for intercourse between the human and divine worlds…[2]

They also believed that exotic metals came into this world from the world of the divine and were brought into it by fire. Hephaestus was the fire god, but he was also the only working god, a blacksmith, and a master craftsman. He was the consummate artist and also a storyteller. According to Homer, when Hephaestus forged Achilles' shield, on the front he inlaid scenes that told stories. One was a city scene:

> The men had gathered in the market-place where, a quarrel was in progress, two men quarrelling over the blood-money for a man who had been killed: one claimed that he was making full compensation, and was showing it to the people, but the other refused to accept any payment: both were eager

to take a decision from the arbiter. The people were taking sides, and shouting their support for either man, while the heralds tried to keep them in check.[3]

Many other ancient Greek craftsmen were also involved in storytelling. For example, scenes from all the ancient myths were depicted on vases and frescos.[4] The fact that craft was so intimately ingrained in storytelling, and in particular the smithy as a place for storytelling, gives us a metaphor for characterizing the author's workplace. All writers are craftsmen and are frequently referred to as "wordsmiths." Therefore, it is natural to call a novelist a "novelsmith" and his craft "novelsmithing."

But many would-be novelsmiths of today want to skip the apprenticeship necessary to learn a craft and jump immediately into getting the words on the page. So it is that frequently the lump of gold they stumble across while living their lives presents itself as a story, and they believe it just might be the next New York Times bestseller, once they've pounded it into the shape of a novel. Shouldn't be that difficult, they think, but fifty pages or so into the writing of it, they lose their way. Seems they've not found a pot of gold at all, but fools gold instead. This comes as a shock, and for many, it constitutes the end of their short experiment with novel writing. But some will be interested enough to seek out a little knowledge about the craft and may even come to view learning about it as interesting as writing a novel. But where can the beginning novelsmith turn to learn his craft?

Good primers on creative writing fill the bookshelves, and heaven knows, a beginning writer would do well to study them thoroughly. But none of these books actually get down to the specifics of putting a novel together. This book, *Novelsmithing,* fills that void.

Novelsmithing provides the beginning novelist, or perhaps even the experienced novelist who has lost his way, with a discussion of the underlying structure and methods of novel writing. It is intended that the reader proceed by taking each chapter in sequence, since the concepts developed in succeeding chapters depend strongly on those coming before.

This approach to novel writing is original, although it does make use of concepts developed by other authors. In particular, I've appropriated the concept of the Premise as developed by Lajos Egri in his *The Art of Dramatic Writing*, although I do take exception to some of his understanding of what constitutes the Premise. My development is a complete approach to structuring a novel so that it forms a consistent and interrelated whole. In addition, I relate the Premise to elements of the analytical psychologist Carl Jung's interpretation of what goes on within the human psyche. As a matter of fact, the entire development has been heavily influenced by Jung's thinking, and in particular, his revelations concerning ancient Greek myth.

The completion of the first nine chapters should provide the author with a rough draft for his novel. Chapter 10 provides him with insight into his own creative processes. Chapter 11 gets into the sticky subject of ethics, and Chapters 12 and 13 provide some basic guidance concerning the editing and publishing of the completed novel.

The ideas developed in this book concern basic storytelling and can just as easily be apply to narrative non-fiction, drama, and screenwriting. My travelogue, *Oedipus on a Pale Horse*, is an example of how a writer might use this technique to generate an extended personal-history narrative.

Author's Note: Origins

I have always been a student of the creative process. During my early years in college, I was introduced to the work of Dostoevsky. I read of all his novels, short stories and a couple of biographies. From this man and his bizarre work, I became interested in writing and made my own first attempts at poetry and fiction.

Also during these initial college years, I was introduced to and fell in love with Greek tragedy. Sophocles had a major impact on me. From the story of Oedipus, I found my way to Freud and the "Oedipus Complex." I read Freud's *Interpretation of Dreams*.

It wasn't until I turned thirty that I actually began work on a novel, and I was still as interested in the creative process as I was in the actual writing. There might be a certain amount of truth in the statement that I started writing to learn about the creative process. I instinctively realized that it spoke to something basic about the human condition. But I aborted my first novel after a hundred pages or so because I didn't know where it was going. I ran out of story. I was puzzled about my failure, and wondered why the story didn't reveal itself to me as I imagined it would.

Several years after this failed attempt, I started and finished another novel, but I knew it was rather rambling and not properly plotted. I attended some workshops on plotting and came away even more confused. I started reading books on screen writing and drama because they seemed to know more about the structure of storytelling. I came across the concept of the Premise, and the plotting process I would later use myself started to take shape.

During this time, I read the comments of other authors concerning the nature of the writing experience. The interviews in *The Paris Review* were my primary source. A little later in life, I went through five years of psychotherapy; and following this trying but illuminating experience, one of the most important events of my life occurred. My company laid me off. Instead of trying to find work immediately, I decided to spend my time reading about ancient Greece, and planned an extended trip about the Greek mainland and islands. Prior to leaving, I read everything I could get my hands on concerning the archaeology and mythology of ancient Greece. At the same time, I planned to use my newly developed plotting methods while writing an extended narrative of my journey through Greece.

I spent ten weeks traveling Greece alone. When I returned, I edited and expanded my travel narrative into the work I've had on the Internet for the last eight years and I recently published in paperback. It's titled *Oedipus on a Pale horse* and is now available on Amazon.

Afterward, I continued my research into the religion and myths of ancient Greece. My primary resources were the writings of university professors, classicists published by university presses. Early in this period, I came into contact with the writings of Karl Kerényi and Carl Jung. I had always known of Jung's work because of his association with Freud, but I had never explored his writings to any extent. I had viewed him, naive as I was, as Freud's junior partner. Surprisingly enough, I had never heard of Kerényi. These two would become my newfound heroes. This research was really exciting because I realized that I was uncovering the psychology of writing.

Freud had always been highly interesting, but Jung's theory of the human psyche interested me even more. I'd had many experiences during my life that had gone unexplained, even through the five years of therapy. Jung came as a revelation. His explanation of the connection between human events and mythology was simply mind-blowing. Karl Kerényi was a professor of classics and the history of religion. He wrote a series of books in association with Carl Jung on the archetypes from Greek mythology that served the ancients as patterns for human existence. Through the writings of these two, I delved deeper into this crossover field of psychology and mythology, and ran onto the archetypal psychologists James Hillman and Murray Stein. It was as if I'd found the Rosetta Stone for my own psychology, as well as a guide into the internal creative process of writing.

Then in the fall of 1999, I was approached by the head of the Continuing Education Department at New Mexico State University at Carlsbad to teach a couple of courses. She'd heard that I was a writer and interested in mythology. "Something on novel writing and Greek mythology," she said, "would be of interest to our older students."

I was already primed. Since most of the students, who would be taking these courses, were college educated, some even retired teachers, I could treat the material as if I were teaching graduate school. My years of research could be put to good use. The course on Greek mythology, I taught primarily from the writings of Homer, Hesiod, Aeschylus, Sophocles, and Euripides. For the novel writing course, I pulled from everything I'd read through the years concerning storytelling: novelists, playwrights, screenwriters, and narrative non-fiction writers. I injected good doses of Jungian and archetypal psychology.

While developing the material for the two courses, I continued to be amazed at how connected the two subjects are, that novel writing, all storytelling really, is an outgrowth of the same psychological processes that had, through the millennia, created myth. Jungian psychology goes a long ways toward explaining the techniques used by novelists, playwrights, and screenwriters. All my research into these different disciplines came together as a sort of critical mass, which resulted in an explosion of ideas concerning the craft of novel writing that I describe here.

My methodology is not the traditional approach used in creative writing. I will not tell you how to combine the words to make effective sentences and paragraphs or to describe a scene. That is taught in many wonderful textbooks and classes in schools throughout the world. But what you will not find in these classes is how to actually put a novel together. This deficiency I hope to correct with *Novelsmithing*.

NOVELSMITHING

The Structural Foundation
of Plot, Character, and Narration

The Psychic Origins of Myth,
the Mythic Origins of Storytelling

CHAPTER 1: The Big Idea

Seems as though everyone has a big idea that they believe will make a great novel. Some of them may be right, but generally ideas that come to a novice constitute only a tiny part of the entire concept that constitutes an idea for a novel. When I lived in Boulder, Colorado, I had a physicist friend who had a Ph.D. come to me with an idea. He imagined, he said, that a man found a suitcase with a million dollars inside an airport bathroom stall. The man would be obsessed with the money and what to do with it. But the physicist couldn't write the story beyond the first fifty pages. "There are too many possibilities," he said. "How do I know what this guy will do with the money?" Actually, my friend had described an interesting situation, but he didn't have a full-blown idea for a novel.

It takes a multitude of ingredients to formulate a full novel concept. The ingredients involve not only situations, but also characters, conflicts, settings, and above all theme. In my friend's situation, his character could have taken the suitcase along with the money to the police, walked away, and it would have had no impact on his life at all. But his character could also have taken it home and come into conflict with the owner, possibly a drug dealer. He could also have immediately purchased an airline ticket, flown to a foreign country and disappeared into the countryside.

The Big Idea

The possibilities are endless, and the final choice of what to do with the money will say something crucial about character and theme. So how do you formulate a story that has all the elements orchestrated so that it constitutes a fine piece of literature?

Janet Burroway, in her book *Writing Fiction* (probably the best book ever written on the subject) says that:

> The organic unity of a work of literature cannot be taught--or, if it can, I have not discovered a way to teach it. I can suggest from time to time that concrete image is not separate from character, which is revealed in dialogue and point of view, which may be illuminated by simile, which may reveal theme, which is contained in plot as water is contained in an apple. But I cannot tell you how to achieve this...[5]

The process I have developed does precisely this.

The many books on novel writing are little more than a hodgepodge of ideas about the subject, but what we will do here gets down to revealing the secrets of where it comes from and how to put it all together. What you will need first is a description of the underlying structure that makes all novels work, the DNA of a novel, so to speak.

So, where do you begin? How do you determine the structure of your story beforehand? How are the infinity of elements related? All of these questions, I will answer shortly, but first, we must get some preliminaries out of the way.

THE NOVEL: What is it?
The *Oxford English Dictionary* defines the novel as:

The Big Idea

> A fictitious prose narrative or tale of considerable length (now usually one long enough to fill one or more volumes), in which characters and actions representative of the real life of past or present times are portrayed in a plot of more or less complexity.

I would also include the real life of future times in this definition, so as to cover science fiction. I would argue that the word "fictitious" may not always apply, because many historical novels are more historically accurate than are some history texts. Milan Kundera, the great Czech novelist, has had it said about his novels that they are "a meditation on existence,"[6] which really leaves the subject wide open.

A novel does not present real life, but it does bear a relationship to it. Some say it is an "illusion of life." Or it can be approached even more casually, as in Henry James' statement that "A novel is of its very nature an 'ado,' an ado about something, and the larger the form it takes the greater of course the ado."[7] I would define the novel as: an extended dramatic narration concerning a particular subject or event. I put forth these definitions to illustrate how ambiguous and flexible the novel art form is. And although I'll give you specific instructions here on how to discover and structure your story, please realize that what you create may be something no one has ever seen before, and have an original structure.

NOVEL TYPE

Novels come in many forms, and the technique described here can be used to create any of them. They may be science fiction, mystery, romance, western, true crime, thriller, historical. Your novel can be mainstream or literary fiction, a children's story or young adult. Literary fiction is more character based than mainstream, which is plot based. Know where your novel will fit among the multitude. Who is your audience? You must be writing for someone. Who is it? An author, first and foremost, should read. All these things, the author should know and do before he starts writing. Part of learning the craft is to know how others practice it and what they produce as a final product.

Some writers have broken down the techniques available to the novelist as equal parts "method and madness," and this concept will be useful to us. The way an author constructs his novel, the craft, is the "method." Where all the raw material comes from, the original idea, characters and events, narrative style, etc., is the "madness." We will study craft first. We'll say a little about where the idea for a novel, the initial impulse, comes from. But this will be fairly basic stuff, and I'll leave the rest until later, when we'll do what we can about studying the "madness."

THE CENTRAL IDEA

The idea for the novel can come from anywhere. Sometimes the idea will come from some traditional story, an action drawn from life, or a personal fantasy. It can come from personal experience, or be completely imaginary, as was my friend's fantasy about the man finding a suitcase. It can be built around a single character, as in Dostoevsky's *Crime and Punishment*, or an event, as in Tom Clancy's *The Hunt for Red October*. It should be something you know about or are willing to learn about through extensive research. One of the best places to find an idea is in your own personal fantasies, especially those involving conflict. Dreams, particularly recurring dreams, are an excellence source. Some experts will advise you to write the type of novel you enjoy reading, but my opinion is that reading and writing are radically different activities. Write what you want to write.

Some writers borrow from other authors. Shakespeare rarely had an original storyline. Many times, he borrowed from Plutarch's *Lives*. (Plutarch was a Greek who wrote in the 2nd century AD.) *A Midsummer Night's Dream* came from *Theseus,* and *Coriolaneus* came from Plutarch's biography of the ancient Greek hero. Jane Smiley took the storyline for *A Thousand Acres* from Shakespeare's *King Lear* and won a Pulitzer. *Cinderella* has been disguised and retold countless times. Gothic novels are of that nature. *Jane Eyre*, *Rebecca*, the movie *Working Girl* are all Cinderella stories.

Other sources might include a personal event, family history, or something that happened to a friend. The TV series "Law and Order" frequently uses a story "ripped from a newspaper headline." But the most original material will come from personal experience. If you are on the outlook for an idea, it can come from anywhere. Consider the origin of Henry James' novel, *The Spoils of Poynton*, which I've included as Attachment I. The idea came to him suddenly during an evening meal and was provoked by an innocent comment by a woman sitting next to him.

HIGH CONCEPT

If a blacksmith took an expensive piece of metal into his furnace, worked the bellows till he was blue in the face and the metal glowing white hot, and then beat on it with his hammer and tongs until it had a unique shape, you'd expect that shape to be something useful or a least something an observer could identify. But if everyone who saw it said, "What is it?" the blacksmith would be pressed into the embarrassing task of explaining what he had created. The same is true for the novelsmith. He would be well advised to create a novel with subject matter that a potential reader can identify with a minimum of scrutiny. It should immediately "resonate" with the reader.

People in publishing today (and particularly in Hollywood) are looking for works that are "high concept." By this they mean that the main subject or essence of the work can be clearly exposed in a few words. Think of ways to express your idea so that it is immediately understandable. The statement will most likely expose the central conflict and say something about the storyline. Dostoevsky's *Crime and Punishment* might be identified as, "A young man's attempt to come to terms with himself after committing murder." If you can't summarize your story in one sentence, you probably don't know what your own novel is about. We'll cover how to do this in detail in the next chapter.

Writing a novel is always accomplished in the dark and is very much a process of discovery. Never mind that you have your computer screen brightness on maximum, the place your material comes from is dark and foreboding. Plus, you really don't know the story until you've written it. Yet, you can't structure it properly until you know the story. Because of this Catch 22, you must write it and rewrite it several times. To begin with, you must have the germ of an idea. Trying to apply a story structure to it will help it develop. If the idea is the art, the structure is the craft.

ART THROUGH CRAFT

The idea for a novel is like a wild horse. You have to harness it to get it under control and discipline it. Your novel will develop as you write, but you will always feel as though you are riding your horse in the dark with a little lantern to show the way. That's why you need to work within a structure that can throw that much-needed light on the subject matter and reveal where it's leading you. In the following pages, I will present a method for developing your idea. It will result in a first draft, so that a full novel can be written from it. Don't be deluded into believing that this is the only way to write a novel. This method, however, will help you understand the energy inherent in any novel, and how it may be harnessed. You can then go out on your own to find unusual ways to structure your novel.

The idea, particularly if it comes from true-life experience, must undergo a transformation before it becomes a novel. Because storytelling is such a part of our lives, we think of it as a representation of life itself, but a novel has certain characteristics that take it out of the real world. In fact, the existence of any story is outside real life. As shown in Figure 1, a transformation process takes place during the creation of the novel.

Figure 1

This transformation is the craft of novel writing. Much of it will be identical to the ordinary storytelling we do everyday when someone asks, "How did it go at the office?" But further realize that the process is not simply a description of real-life events. A transformation takes place when we take "real-life" into the world of the novel, and that transformation occurs through craft. As an example, conversation is transformed into "dialogue" to sound

The Big Idea

"normal" within a novel. Dialogue is an abbreviated or edited version of normal conversation. Everything is magnified and has a storyline connection; therefore, the author has to develop a new set of proportions to judge the impact of his words on the reader.

"But," you may say, "I don't want to be a craftsman. I want to be an artist." Craft is the method, the discipline, of dealing with all artistic endeavors. The artist, the author, must learn his craft to get his ideas into the fictional world. Art, for some reason, doesn't want to be criticized or reviewed, perhaps because it is so ego-related. On the other hand, craftsmanship by its very nature implies an apprenticeship, a period of trial and failure, and a certain level of skill before becoming a master craftsman. Viewing novel writing, novelsmithing, as a craft takes the pressure off your initial efforts, and opens them up to critique. Plus, it means that, to learn to write, you must write, write, write until you get it right.

I use the metaphor of a blacksmith for the novelist because a blacksmith is the consummate craftsman. He gets as down and dirty as any and more than most. Plus his tools, anvil and hammer, tongs, bellows, are coarse, heavy tools, and his actions, the swing of the hammer, the whoosh of the bellows, ring throughout the countryside. This is in opposition to the actions of the novelsmith, who sits quietly at his computer, only the faint click of the keys audible above his own breathing. By viewing novel writing as smithing, we can exaggerate the novelsmith's actions to better see their complexity and gauge their importance, and to help us keep our focus on the craft.

The blacksmith is not the only metaphor that we'll use to uncover the craft of novel writing. We'll use other analogies as appropriate. Some may criticize the metaphor mixing, but we'll play it loose and shoot from the hip when necessary.

The Big Idea

★

That concludes the introductory remarks. To follow the discussion from here on, you should have an idea for the novel you wish to write. You will be developing that idea into a rough draft. But the central most important fact you should retain from this introduction is that the real world and the fictional world are radically different, and that you can only get your story into the fictional world through narrative craft.

EXERCISES

(a) Before proceeding to the next chapter, write down your own concept, your idea, for your novel. (b) List two or three of the major characters. This will help define the core of your idea, so that it it can be further fleshed out in the next chapter.

CHAPTER 2: Plot

Just as most of the metals with which a blacksmith works are amalgams and alloys, a novel is generally said to have three constituents: plot, characterization, and setting.[8] Plot is the author's contrivance of storyline, its narrative structure. Characterization is the act of establishing identity, creating the 'people' populating the novel. Setting is the location wherein the novel takes place, and includes landscape as well as atmosphere, and mood or tone. The internal landscape of a character is also tremendously important as a "setting." But the essence of a novel goes beyond these constituents. A novel is an organic whole, a living being, so to speak. Not only was Hephaestus the god of fire, who made armor for Achilles, he was also the craftsman who created the first woman, Pandora. The novelsmith should also view the creation of his novel as the creation a living thing. Everything in it contributes to its life. What doesn't contribute to that life doesn't belong, and should be removed. As Aristotle stated 2300 years ago:

> [The story] must represent one action, a complete whole, with its several incidents so closely connected that the transposition or withdrawal of any one of them will disjoin and dislocate the whole. For that which makes no perceptible difference by its presence or absence is no real part of the whole.[9]

Plot

That pretty well isolates the story from everything not part of it. And you can keep most of the extraneous material from ever getting into your novel by knowing your entire storyline, doing all the plotting, before you start writing.

You might say that the initial plotting is a little like the blacksmith, or perhaps the metallurgist before him, taking the raw ore and heating it in his hearth until the pure metal separates from the slag. If you don't do this work early, all the impurities you leave in will weaken your storyline and compromise the final work.

To expand a little, plot is the author's ordered contrivance of storyline in the interest of furthering the reader's emotional and intellectual experience. Plotting is a lengthy process, much of which will occur while writing the novel, but the bulk should be done up front before you put any of the actual words on paper. Avoid the temptation to start writing when you first get an idea. Holding off until you thoroughly know your entire storyline allows you to be on top of the story instead of totally within it. This gives the author perspective and the confidence to write with authority. Delaying the writing also minimizes mistakes, ensures that the author knows what to put in and leave out, but more importantly, it stores the creative energy so it can explode on the page. As the novelsmith, you can swing your hammer with confidence. Plotting allows you to develop story strategy as opposed to simply supplying a sequence of events littered with facts. Plotting up front separates the metal from the slag.

So how do you get a handle on this plotting process? The answer is that every story has a kernel from which everything else builds.

Plot

THE SECRET BEHIND PLOTTING

The first step in plotting is to establish the core of the story around which everything will evolve. This central core is known in the industry as the Premise.

> Definition: Premise, a proposition to be proved; a basis of argument.

Premise is the Rosetta Stone for decoding the entire idea and getting it into the form of a novel. A Premise forms the core of every meaningful story. In the same spirit as the proverbial grain of sand that contains the history of the universe, so the Premise contains the motivating force behind everything in the novel, and is the author's guiding light for what to put in and leave out.[10]

Since the Premise is the "seed" from which your novel will grow, it contains the genetic material for the entire tree. Only then will it have a strong trunk (storyline), develop branches (subplots), flower (generate ideas), and in the end, bear fruit (prove its point). Henry James explained the effect of having a good Premise this way:

> One's luck was to have felt one's subject right—whether [by] instinct or calculation...; and the circumstance even amounts perhaps to a little lesson that when this has happily occurred faults may show, faults may disfigure, and yet not upset the work. It remains in equilibrium by having found its centre, the point of command of all the rest. From this centre the subject has been treated, from this centre the interest has spread, and so, whatever else it may do or may not do, the thing has acknowledged a principle of composition and con-

trives to at least hang together.[11]

James' statement emphasizes the point that every story should be more than just a sequence of events. It must have the intellectual core that will hold it together, a core that provides meaning. We'll discuss "meaning" in more detail later, but keep in mind that every novel has a point to make. Any event that sticks in your mind does so for a reason, and that reason is that it means something to you. What, you may not quite be able to articulate, but it does.

Henry James aside, all this has undoubtedly started to degenerate into obscurities that you can't quite see how to put into practice, so let's set this rather philosophical discussion aside and make it really simple. The Premise in its essence is *conflict*. And conflict can be expressed in three words:

X versus Y
Example: Good overcomes Evil

Again, first and foremost, Premise is about conflict. That's what sets the forces in motion (starts the novel) and leads to resolution (ends the novel). You must have a Premise to have a novel at all. Until you have one, you're just stoking a dead fire. Hidden within the Premise are both main characters and the central conflict. This may sound startling, but it's the nature of conflict. Conflict occurs because of opposing wills. These "wills" may be two individuals, two families (as in a family feud), two countries (as in war), etc. The possibilities are endless. If you want an image for the Premise: two bighorn sheep butting heads during rut.

My friend with the character who found a suitcase of money couldn't find his story because he didn't have a Premise. No one

15

opposed his character's desire to keep the money. If he brought in a drug lord, he'd be in business.

The reason I say that you should first have an idea for a novel is that it's practically impossible to start with a Premise; the Premise is ambiguous by nature. If you have an idea for a novel first, then you can use the principle behind the Premise to uncover the hidden elements and fully develop it into a well-rounded story.

If the Premise is viewed as the key, then the idea is the locked door that must be opened to expose all the elements of the story. Using this key, the first word of the Premise gives us the protagonist, the third the antagonist. The second word contains the conflict and its result. These three elements are immediately revealed through examination of the Premise. Since novels are about conflict, the conflict must be "locked" early in the story, thus setting the characters in motion. Some movie makers are so anxious to lock the conflict that they do so before the titles roll. The story ends when the conflict is resolved.

AN EXAMPLE

As an example, let's say you want to write a novel about a young woman who loves children. As far as this idea goes, it isn't a story because it has no conflict. It has a character, possibly the protagonist, but no story. If you further state that the woman can't have children because she is sterile, we then at least have conflict. The woman's emotional needs are in conflict with her biological state, and we have the beginning of a story, although we don't yet have a full Premise, because we don't know the nature of her biological problem and how she overcomes or succumbs to her physical limitations. If you say that she is sterile because her husband forced her to have surgery, we have uncovered more of the

Premise because we know the antagonist, the husband, but we still don't know the outcome. If you say that she divorces her husband, has her surgery reversed, and has a child by artificial insemination, then we have a full story.

I'll not go into the multitude of possible Premises inherent in this simple story, but I will provide a couple of attempts at defining it. A very simple Premise might be "wife overcomes husband," which is character-oriented. "Good overcomes evil" is another possible Premise, and this time it is cosmic in its scope. A further possibility is "determination overcomes control," which is psychology related. The main thing you should get from this example is how to work with a Premise to develop your idea.

At this point, you might want to consider other novels, movies or plays you admire to determine whether you can uncover a possible Premise for each. Remember that the Premise is a working tool for the craftsman. It insures that your efforts are rewarded by a full-bodied story.

PREMISE POSSIBILITIES

With this example behind us, let's look at some possibilities for a Premise. Keep in mind that conflict creates a tension that gives the story an inevitable sense of forward motion and puts on the brakes when it is resolved at the end. Here are some examples of a "three-word" Premise:

1. Intelligence overcomes stupidity.
2. Anarchy overcomes order.
3. Forbidden love destroys the lovers. (Romeo and Juliet?)
4. Jealousy destroys the person. (Othello?)
5. Unbridled ambition destroys the person. (Macbeth?)

6. Faith conquers pride.
7. Intelligence overcomes superstition.
8. Procrastination destroys the person. (Hamlet?)
9. Poverty destroys society.
10. Love overcomes hatred.

The order of each of these, and thus the outcome, could be reversed. The number of possibilities is endless.

The Premise not only provides conflict, but also takes sides in that conflict. By doing this, the Premise provides meaning and exposes an underlying truth, or what the author believes to be a truth. And now we come to one of the great paradoxes of novel writing:

The Premise is never specifically stated.

The Premise, although it is the "be all and end all" of storytelling, will never be explicitly stated in the novel. If it is stated explicitly, you will be preaching to your reader. The reader must be left on his own to form his opinion of what the subject matter means. The author can only go so far down the road to get his meaning across.

To make sure you understand the concept of Premise, let's approach the origin of your Premise one more time:

Question: How and where do you find your Premise?
Answer: You must uncover the Premise from within your idea for the novel.

The idea will usually, but not always, come first. You'll pull some event from your life experience or elsewhere, and then start looking for meaning and a Premise. The Premise will seem trivial, but it will take on greater significance within the full context of the novel. As you develop all the elements, you should always return to the Premise for guidance. You will get tired of thinking about Premise before it is all over, but don't let your irritation get the better of you. Your ability to handle the Premise will either make or break you as a novelsmith.

EXAMPLES FROM STORIES WE ALL KNOW

The conflict can be internal to a single individual, as in Dostoeveky's *Crime and Punishment*. Raskolnikov is in conflict with himself. He eventually turns himself in for murdering two sisters. In the movie *Groundhog Day*, the Premise might be stated as: "man overcomes his own base nature," or in three words: "man overcomes himself." One might suppose God is the teacher giving Phil the chance to live one day over and over until he gets it right. Phil's conflict is with himself. He can't get past his own base self to win the girl he loves.

It can be a conflict between two rights (which turns out to be the most philosophically profound) as in the Dustin Hoffman/Meryl Streep movie *Kramer vs. Kramer*. Both parents love their child and have a right to custody. Note that the conflict is expressed in this movie's title and that it relates to the Premise. But it doesn't tell the outcome, so it isn't the Premise. So what is the Premise? Could it be "altruism overcomes personal need"? That might be it for Meryl Streep's character, but I'm sure you can come up with many more that apply.

Since the Premise is about conflict between opposing wills, let's say a few words about what does not fit this pattern. Frequently, we hear adventure stories expressed as "man versus the mountain." But a mountain has no will, so this is not even a true conflict. A man or woman struggling to climb a mountain is struggling against his or her own will and physical limitations. This is an internal struggle, and can be covered by Premise quite easily as "man overcomes himself." You might say that the will to continue overcomes the desire to turn back. In this same vein, "man overcomes lion" is a worthy Premise, because a lion has a will and can stalk the man just the same as can a serial killer.

Remember that the Premise will expose character and the nature of the conflict, as well as dictate the beginning and end of the story. It exposes character because the individuals who are in conflict care deeply about what they are in conflict over. The way they deal with the conflict, i.e., whether they want to argue or grab a gun, exposes character. The story starts when the conflict is locked, and ends when it is resolved.

The Premise may, and usually does, raise a question of universal significance. The movie *Star Wars* has a cosmic landscape because of "The Force," and has universal significance because of the struggle between good and evil. The universal question raised concerns the relationship between good and evil. Which is the most powerful? Which is the right path to follow? The universal comes from the particular. Luke, the embodiment of "good," is a single human being engaged in a battle against Darth Vader, the embodiment of the "evil" or "dark side" of the Force.

A Premise will exist for each sub-conflict (subplot) in the novel. This then defines what a subplot is: a secondary conflict between opposing wills. All subplots must also be resolved by the end of the novel. This is what we commonly call "tying up all the loose ends." Realizing that each subplot is essentially a conflict that must be locked in the beginning (or close to it) and resolved at the end (or close to it) provides the author with a handle to manage all the sub-conflicts.

Something that may not be immediately obvious is that Premise always, at least on a metaphoric level, connotes cosmic forces at work and provides the spiritual level necessary to insure you'll capture the full human experience. It may contain a moral, although that is not necessary. It may be optimistic, pessimistic, or simply state the way the world works. In the movie *Titanic*, the cosmic conflict is "God destroys arrogance." This conflict is locked when Cal (Rose's fiancé) says, "Even God couldn't sink the Titanic." The principle human conflict in the story is between Rose and Cal. Rose is the protagonist, Cal the antagonist. This conflict is locked when Rose boards the Titanic and likens it to a slave ship with she herself being taken aboard in chains. The Premise for this conflict is "freedom overcomes bondage." The word "freedom" tells us a lot about Rose as a character. We know she craves freedom above all else. The word "bondage" also tells us a lot about her mother and her fiancé. They believe Rose should bow to society's demands and their own requirements of her. The word "overcomes" also tells us the ending of the story. We know Rose will escape to live her life to its fullest. The screenwriter knows the outcome before he starts writing, but the audience will only learn the full nature of the Premise at the end.

The Premise is elusive, and your impression of it may change throughout the development of the novel. Still, you need to make a guess at the start to organize your material and develop a complete storyline. Writing a novel is an iterative process. That's why having a synopsis before starting the actual writing of the novel is crucial. The synopsis is the first cut at the complete storyline.

Plot

A quick word about Premise and its relationship to Jungian psychology, since you might have the feeling that we've gone a bit far afield. You can rest assured that Premise does have its roots in Jungian psychology, as I will describe in detail in Chapter 10, "Psychology of Creativity." As a preview, I'll say that the source of creativity within us is hidden away in the subconscious. Access to this portion of the psyche is through a gate guarded by a "presence" that is in conflict with our conscious self. This internal conflict is voiced though the projection of conflict into our thoughts and daily activities; it wants all these conflicts resolved through a process known as "talking it to death." Throughout eternity, this internal process has manifested in storytelling. Our conscious selves, together with the contrary presence standing at the gateway into the subconscious, and the argument that ensues, has the essence of Premise.

STORY MILESTONES

Now that we have defined the Premise, which gives us the principal characters, identifies the primary conflict, and provides the beginning and ending of the novel, we can start to uncover more of the novel's structure. First of all, a novel is a little like a life, and this metaphor isn't so far afield from our blacksmith analogy, because a novel is immortal. It lives long after the novelsmith has passed away. In ancient Greece, fire was known for its immortality producing effects. I'll provide a single reference to illustrate this. In the *Homeric Hymn to Demeter*, the goddess Demeter places Demophoon, a mortal child, in the hearth fire to make him immortal, but Metaneira, the child's mother, catches the goddess doing this and screams in protest, not understanding the goddess's intent. So the novelsmith's hearth seems to be the correct place for the birth of a novel. The apparent paradox is that, though the novel suffers a death in that it does end, it lives eternally, or at least as long as one book exists. Conflict and adversity are these "fires of life" that produce immortality. The Premise can then be viewed as the fire within the novelsmith's forge.

So let's look at a life to uncover the analogous elements that might tell us something about the novel. Life has a beginning (birth) and an ending (death). The birth of a novel is locking the conflict through the coming together of the protagonist and the antagonist, a little like the sperm and the egg. The end of the novel, through conflict resolution, is its death. The story is over, finished, its life expended. This, then, is the basic structure of a novel.

But, we can further expand the structure. Remember in what follows that the Premise never appears as an explicit part of the novel. The Premise is the unseen force driving it. Structure comes from the natural elements of storytelling. Applying it to your idea will open it up and reveal the depth of your own story.[12]

THE NOVEL DIAGRAM

To help visualize the structure of a novel, all the major plot events and resulting actions are shown in Figure 2 and explained in the following narrative.

a. Beginning: Putting the Characters in Motion

First thing on the agenda is to lock the conflict. The modern American novel will generally have some event at the beginning that puts the main characters in conflict, and thus, sets them in motion. You might say that this activates the Premise. Some call this "the hook," because it hooks, or engages, the reader's interest, but this term doesn't necessarily relate to conflict or define the relationship of the initial "hook" to the rest of the story. Locking the central conflict defines the scope of the story, and the hook better accomplish this or it is superfluous. To the extent that the conflict is delayed from the start of the narrative, the reader will puzzle over what the story is about, and thus, whether or not he is interested.[13]

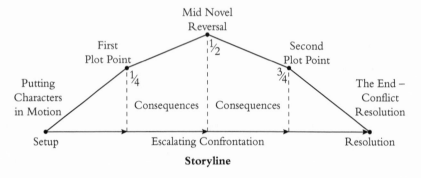

Figure 2

b. First Plot Point

One quarter of the way into the novel, a major event occurs that deepens the conflict and takes the story in a new direction, a direction in which the story will continue for the rest of the novel. It exposes the true nature of the central conflict. It will be an unexpected addition to the storyline and renew the reader's interest. This constitutes the end of the beginning. Nothing really new about the plot will be introduced from here on. All the main characters must be on stage at this point. In *Groundhog Day*, the first plot point occurs when Phil wakes the second morning to find that the holiday is repeating. This is the first plot point, and the rest of the movie follows that format. In the movie *Titanic*, this is where Rose contemplates suicide while standing over the railing at the edge of the ship.

The concept of a "First Plot Point" has a rather remarkable connection with ancient Greek religion. The ancient Greeks realized that life is punctuated by a few major events, such as puberty, that constitute life transitions. Cult initiation ceremonies within the ancient religion defined the nature of these events, and helped the initiate make the life transition. For the women of Attica, this took the form of a symbolic death ritual at puberty, which was held at Brauron on the eastern coast. The girls "danced the Bear" and sacrificed a she-goat that represented their maiden selves. This was the transformation of the maiden into full womanhood, and was visualized as the death of the maiden she had been and as well as her rebirth as a young woman. She was still the same person, but transformed. You might say she'd reached the end of the beginning of her life.

Using the analogy of a novel as a life would then mean that the novel should also undergo this transformation, if it is to become fully formed and adult in scope. The conflict locked in the beginning must be transformed into one of greater significance, thus forcing greater character involvement. Just as ancient women underwent the initiation at puberty, the one-quarter point of their life, so the novel will undergo this conflict transformation at the one-quarter point. This is "the end of the beginning," and as the confrontation escalates for the next quarter of the novel, the characters play out the consequences of Plot Point 1.

c. Mid-Novel Reversal

Perhaps the most difficult task for the beginning and advanced storyteller is preventing the mid-novel sag. A novel is a long narrative art form, and reader interest can only be maintained by constant change. This means that the nature of the conflict, not just the intensity of it, must also change. Some changes in the storyline will be greater than others, and this is one of the largest changes. But this change isn't anything artificial that must be superimposed on the novel structure. This reversal occurs because of the nature of prolonged conflict. In a short story, this change may not be present at all. A long story undergoes a subtle but profound change halfway through. Generally, this will be a reversal in the primary conflict. One might say that the reason a long story has a tendency to sag in the middle is that the storyteller isn't fully aware of the nuances in his storyline. Said another way, the reason a certain story may be long is that it has this reversal at its midpoint.

Up until the midpoint, one character, protagonist or antagonist, will be the aggressor. After it, the opposite character will be the aggressor. In *Titanic*, the ship floats for the first half of the movie (the builders represent the aggressor), but right in the middle of the movie, it hits an iceberg and sinks for the second half of the movie (God is the aggressor). In James Fenimore Cooper's *The Last of the Mohicans*, the Indians chase the white men for the first half of the novel, and the white men chase the Indians for the second half. The writers for the television series *Law and Order* always lock the conflict (usually the discovery the body) before the main actors come on the scene, and they go to the first commercial. One half-hour into the show (the mid point), they always handcuff the suspect, and the police turn the case over to the lawyers. In the movie *Jaws*, the fish chases the people for the first half, and they chase the fish the second half. Everywhere you look, you will find other examples.

Plot

d. Second Plot Point

The second plot point occurs three quarters of the way through the novel. This event leads directly to the resolution of the conflict. This is the point at which one of the opposing forces is revealed to be the stronger, and also when the Premise is confirmed. But it is still a little short of conflict resolution, which occurs at the end. What is absolutely essential here is that the protagonist exhibit "the agony of choice." At this point in *Titanic*, Rose is aboard the lifeboat with her mother, headed for a life of servitude. Suddenly, she comes to her senses, realizes she is making a mistake, and climbs out of the lifeboat and back onto Titanic to be with Jack. Cameron stretches out the scene by swelling the music while Rose agonizes over her decision. Again, she shows her willingness to risk everything to get what she wants. Jack is her symbol of freedom.

When viewing the novel as a life, as we did earlier, the second plot point has a "life" altering impact just as had the first plot point. The novel can now see the end of its life, and it is looking forward, more than ever, to the meaning of it all, but it is also looking backward to pull on what it has learned during its "life." This might be termed the "point of wisdom," because the novel has matured throughout its life, and is now alluding to that truth that lies above itself, that rather divine truth that is only exposed through an ironic stance. The fires of life have had their effect, and the novel is now becoming immortal, though it is about to suffer death in resolution.

Human beings, in the later stages of life, tend to think back on their lives and reminisce through storytelling, to explore their own mythology. The events of the novel have now become myth within the novel itself, and the novel will tend to look back on itself and see the events metaphorically.

e. The End: Conflict Resolution

Novelists (and screenwriters) have no end of problems with endings. Generally, this is because they do not understand their Premise. Premise dictates the outcome at the end. All the elements of the story, including main characters, conflict, setting, have been selected to fulfill the Premise. At the end, one of the two major forces in the novel overcomes the other, according to the dictates of the Premise. This is what is generally called the climax. The author, who has done his plotting well, knows the end of the story before he ever puts pencil to paper, because he believes in his Premise. He may, however, struggle over the way his ending comes about.

f. Denouement

The only thing that may occur after conflict resolution is the revelation of its effects, the denouement. At the end of *Titanic*, we see pictures of Rose throughout her life, depicting all her accomplishments brought about through exercising the freedom of choice she learned about from Jack. If, in the end, Rose had left the dock with Cal, the entire audience would have groaned. Instead, she hid her face from Cal and turned away. James Cameron knew the end of the movie before he wrote the screenplay. I'd bet my house on it.

One of the most famous endings of all novels is in Fitzgerald's *The Great Gatsby*. Gatsby's world has collapsed, and he killed in a case of mistaken identity perpetrated by Gatsby's girlfriend's husband. Nick, the narrator of Gatsby's story, ruminates over what has happened:

> And as I sat there brooding on the old, unknown world, I thought of Gatsby's wonder when he first picked out the green light at the end of Daisy's dock. He had come a long way to this blue lawn, and his dream must have seemed so close that he could hardly fail to grasp it. He did not know that it was already behind him, somewhere back in that vast obscurity beyond the city, where the dark fields of the republic rolled on under the night.
>
> Gatsby believed in the green light, the orgiastic future that year by year recedes before us. It eluded us then, but that's no matter—tomorrow we will run faster, stretch out our arms father.... And one fine morning——
>
> So we beat on, boats against the current, borne back ceaselessly into the past.[14]

Nick has started to reminisce over the events that have unfolded, to draw conclusions, and has developed a philosophy. He sees a truth emerging from what has happened around him and has developed an ironic stance that alludes to a complex truth that can only be seen when the entire novel is viewed as a whole. From his stance above the events at the end of the novel, Nick has gained a certain wisdom that can only be expressed through irony. As Colebrook puts it:

> Perhaps wisdom requires irony: *not* speaking literally and explicitly, recognizing that there is always more to what we say.[15]

This has been Fitzgerald's intent from the beginning: to demonstrate a basic truth about the human condition, which he has formulated with his Premise. At the end, Fitzgerald has resorted to an ironic metaphor, "boats against the current," to convey the philosophical impact of the events on his character.

Fitzgerald has also used dramatic irony because he has given the reader clues so that he might see beyond Nick's insightful comments. Gatsby was never "great." He was, after all, a bootlegger, a drug dealer and wife stealer. He was a common criminal, a gangster really, who was victimized by his own acts. We'll discuss irony in detail in Chapter 5.

PREMISE TRINITY

Every well-written novel will have three levels of Premise, a Premise Trinity. First, there's the cosmic Premise (e.g., good versus evil), then the story Premise (e.g., freedom overcomes bondage), and then the character Premise (e.g., self-determination overcomes society's demands). These are three aspects of the same Premise, although each may have a different outcome. In *Titanic*, the cosmic struggle is between the divine forces of good and evil, and this struggle remains unresolved. The story Premise is the Titanic's struggle to stay afloat. The Titanic loses. The character premise is Rose's attempt to throw off the bonds of her mother and her fiancé and live her own life. Rose wins.

Each subplot could potentially also have a full set of Premises. From this, you can now understand the complexity of a novel's underlying structure, and the reason novels, or any story for that matter, are so variously interpreted. You may also be able to understand the multitude of reasons why so many novels and movies fall short of their promise. Few writers really understand the underlying structure inherent in a novel or screenplay.

Plot

Chances are you've seen all of these movies and read these novels, never realizing the structure underneath. That's the nature of plotting. Story structure disappears behind events, just the same as a home's framework isn't visible under drywall, paint, and texturing. A novelsmith, or any advanced storyteller for that matter, can't afford to operate solely on intuition. That's the reason some novels fail so miserably. The authors haven't built the framework, and actually don't understand the nature of storytelling. But don't paste the storyline artifacts onto your story. Examine your story to uncover these turns of events, and place them where they should occur.

Henry James provides us with another example, this one concerning the plotting of his novel, *The American*, and I've included it as Attachment II. In just a couple of paragraphs, James describes how the idea for the novel came to him, and how he plotted it on the spot. It just goes to show that, when you know your craft, an idea can be turned into a plotted novel almost immediately.

HOW TO ANSWER THE QUESTION:
"What is your novel about?"

This is one of the most frustrating questions a novelist can be asked, and you'd be surprised at how few can provide a good answer. You can answer this question in many ways, and with the description of the novel's structure provided above, you'll be able to come up with several good answers. You may simply state the Premise, provide a short summary of the storyline, or provide a description of your protagonist and/or the antagonist. You may answer on the Premise level by saying that it's about the cosmic struggle between good and evil, for instance. On the story level,

Plot

James Cameron could say that *Titanic* is about the sinking of a great ship. On the character level, he could say that it's about a woman who gains her freedom from family domination. He wouldn't even have to say that she does this while surviving the sinking of the Titanic.

Understanding your Premise provides the tools that will enable you to discuss the essence of your novel with an agent, publisher or publicist. You won't become tongue-tied, as is so frequently the case, when asked, "What is your novel about?"

PERPETUAL CONFLICT

Conflict may be the force that drives the novel forward, but it isn't the be-all and end-all. The blacksmith doesn't apply only fire to get the shape and hardness of the object with which he is working. Even the surface finish may be important, and that can take a little tender love and care. Similarly, applying too much heat to the novelsmith's fire or pounding the conflict too much can cause the destruction of the whole concept. In other words, the conflict doesn't have to be a "to-the-death" struggle. It can be emotional, as in *Kramer vs. Kramer* in which the characters are sympathetic to each other and share a love for their little boy. They resist their lawyers' efforts to get them to destroy each other. It is often said that the most meaningful stories are those in which the conflict is between two rights. Good does not change, nor does evil. The more interesting struggle is between two good characters who are trying to determine the better path to follow, or perhaps, to understand the very nature of goodness. This was the nature of the conflict in *Kramer vs. Kramer*.

Don't get stuck in the "take-no-prisoners" mentality. The conflict may even be obscure as in Arthur C. Clark's *Rendezvous with Rama*, in which the Premise seems to be "Curiosity overcomes Narcissism." In this sci-fi novel, conflict doesn't seem to exist at all. The novel's forward motion appears to be driven solely by discovery. The focus for most of the novel is on the questions: "What's inside the mysterious spaceship entering the solar system," and "Why are these visitors from outer space coming to visit us?" Only at the very end do we realize how narcissistic our perceptions have been, and meaning finally comes to the story when the spaceship dips in close to the sun to scoop up plasma. This act tells us unequivocally that the spaceship is on a fueling run and has no interest in us at all. The conflict, all along, has been between perception and reality. And the resolution comes as a revelation at the very end.

These then are the basics of plotting. Remember that your Premise will many times be obscure, but don't let that fact permit your focus to drift from it. Allow Premise and story structure to focus your material. Once you have a storyline, you can start working earnestly on the narrative technique you'll employ to begin writing the novel. We'll get to narration shortly, but first we need to talk about character development in more detail.

FOUR SENTENCE SUMMARY

1. Storyline gives the novel length.
2. Characters give the novel breadth.
3. Premise gives the novel depth.
4. A novel with these elements is a three-dimensional simulation of life.

EXERCISES
(a) Using the concept for your novel that you wrote down as an exercise at the end of the previous chapter, develop a Premise for the principal conflict. (b) Identify the protagonist and antagonist. (c) List the major events from the Novel Diagram that define the geometry of your novel and provide a short description of each. (d) Write both a one-sentence and a one-paragraph description of the complete storyline. (e) State the central question posed by the Premise.

CHAPTER 3: Character

Character motivations, wishes and desires, are the driving forces behind the novel. Character emotion exerts dramatic pressure on the storyline and forces it forward. Therefore, without interesting, highly motivated characters the novel loses its emotional impact.

The situation is even more critical, however, than just having interesting characters. The reading experience can only become personal through characters. The more intimate the contact with a character, the more the reader will react emotionally. In dramatic fiction, the reader must be allowed to view both the fictional world and feel the human impact of the story. To receive the human impact, the reader must have an affinity for one or more of the characters. The reader then gets a human perspective on events. The character must be someone threatened and pushed about by events. Otherwise the novel becomes little more than a narrative history.

AUTHOR/CHARACTER RELATIONSHIP

The relationship between author and character is fraught with paradox. The author, in a sense, resides within all his characters (and will always absorb some of their neuroses). Ironically, only by getting your characters away from you can you get that closeness needed to relate to them and write them properly. We say to hook up with voice and write from within the character. Approach all your characters through their senses. Listen to them, and let their experience generate your words. If your character climbs on a horse, we need to feel the saddle, smell the leather, and sense the height. In that way, you'll be able to determine what jumps off the page and is "alive," as opposed to that which lingers lifelessly on the page.

As human beings, we know so little about ourselves that we have difficulty relating to a character that we see as ourselves. A good exercise is to write about someone we view as our opposite. This is one of the best ways to identify that hidden part of ourselves that our characters represent. In *Madam Bovary*, Flaubert so completely identified with Emma Bovary that, when he described her suicide, he could taste the arsenic in his own mouth.

> The taste of arsenic was so really in my mouth when I described how Emma Bovary was poisoned, that it cost me two indigestions one upon the other quite real ones, for I vomited my dinner.[16]

Every author strives for that closeness, so much so that many authors feel that they are not creating a character, but channeling one.

READER/CHARACTER RELATIONSHIP

In the next chapter, we'll investigate the role of the narrator, the voice that tells the story. The relationship between reader and narrator is much the same as the relationship between reader and character, but distinct differences sometimes do exist, so it's best to talk about character separately.

In Boris Pasternak's *Doctor Zhivago*, we see the novel's world and its events through the eyes of a poet. He is our "camera to the world;" more than that, we gauge our reaction by the impact events have upon him, and we suffer along with him. This is as it should be. The reader always gives up a part of himself to one or more of the characters in a good novel, and rides piggyback on those characters' feelings. The relationship between reader and character is illustrated in Figure 3:

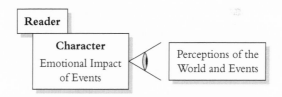

Figure 3.

The reader emotionally attaches to a character and experiences the world and events through him. Only in this way does the novel simulate a real experience instead of just hearsay. It's crucial that the author understand the importance of this. The reader must "experience" the story, and he can only experience the drama vicariously, through a character.

As you'll learn in the next chapter, the reader is in a state of total sensory deprivation, and must have a surrogate who feels and experiences for him in the fictional world. Whenever we, as readers, are deprived of this character contact, the fictional dream dims and we lose interest. The exception, of course, is the occasional use of narrative summary, which does not have to be "experienced," and by way of which information may be received secondhand.

The more plot-driven the story, the more it will seem con-trived. To prevent this, the author must let the characters drive the plot. A character's emotions and wishes exert dramatic pressure on the storyline and force it to flow naturally. Some academics call the storyline the "wish-line." Emotional energy causes things to happen. Emotions produce the intensity and vividness that keep the story interesting. Character feelings stretch along the thread of storyline like pearls strung along a necklace.

CHARACTER CREATION

Through the years, creative writing instructors have described all sorts of ways to create characters. Most suggest writing charac-ter biographies, which is a very good idea, but rarely do they go on to tell you how to ensure that your characters bear the correct relationships to the story. The approach I present here will ensure that the proper relationships are established. As with all elements of the novel, to create characters we return to Premise. As stated before, the first word of the Premise provides the protagonist, and the third word the Antagonist. This is illustrated in Figure 4:

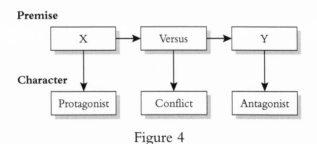

Figure 4

First, a word about the concepts "protagonist" and "antagonist." Commonly referred to, the protagonist is the story's "hero" and the antagonist its "villain." Though these concepts may serve your story well and in some stories even fit the characters perfectly, I find these concepts generally rather naïve. In the best of stories, particularly those that reflect most real-life situations (excluding serial killer stories, etc.), we have no clear-cut heroes or villains. Certainly, neither the mother nor father becomes a villain in *Kramer vs. Kramer*. Webster's Dictionary does a little better, defining protagonist as "one who takes the leading part in a drama," and the antagonist as "one that opposes, an adversary."

Generally, I prefer to refer to the protagonist as the point-of-view character. He's the one the narrator follows around throughout the novel. The antagonist is then the character in conflict with the protagonist. This moves us away from a moral judgment of the two main characters.

We gain more information about each of these central characters by investigating the nature of their conflict. We know that the protagonist feels strongly about what is at stake in the conflict, and that the antagonist feels equally determined about it. Because of their strong affinity for the same thing, the two will be opposites in some ways, and in others, mirror images, but they will always be related.

What is most important is that authors realize the gold mine of character traits that come from the Premise. By selecting the most central aspects of character from the Premise, the author will ensure that the character is directly connected to the storyline and suited to the action resulting from the conflict. This welds Premise (theme), storyline and characterization so as to achieve the unity that Burroway knew a novel had to have, but didn't know how to achieve.

Character

HEART OF CHARACTER

The central, most important characteristics of both the protagonist and antagonist are identified in the Premise. These are
characters in crisis, and the nature of the conflict between them
will define who they are, and help the reader see beyond them
to the level of the primal forces they represent. To illustrate this,
I'll use a rather trite, but exquisite, example from the movie *The
Wizard of Oz*. Each of the characters Dorothy befriends on her
way to see the Wizard has a defect. The scarecrow needs brains,
the Tin Man a heart, and the Cowardly Lion courage. Though this
is a childish implementation of the technique, it illustrates clearly
how to allow the reader to focus, not only on the characters'
physical attributes, which may also be distinctive, but also to give
us a view of the inside of each character and, in doing this, make
them "human." By making these secondary characters an animal,
a mechanical-man, and a gunnysack stuffed with straw, the screenwriters further defined the physical attributes of the characters,
and their way of reacting to the world, at a single brushstroke and
made them easily identifiable to children. As a result of this characterization, the story is loaded with meaning.

In *Titanic*, Rose's central characteristic is a desire for freedom.
The central characteristic of both her mother and her fiancé is
their desire to keep Rose under control, in bondage, though the
motivation of each is different. On the other hand, Jack's intentions toward Rose are for her to become her own person. Rose's
interaction with Jack more fully develops her personality, exposing the depth of her desire for independence and freedom. Her
fiancé's attempts to keep her away from Jack expose the depth
of his desire to control her. Eventually, she comes to risk her life

Character

to save Jack (her symbol of freedom), and her fiancé is driven to attempt murder. This primal struggle between freedom and bondage is then fully manifested in character. Rose's life then becomes the perfect metaphor for the cosmic theme of the human spirit's struggle for freedom.

Another aspect of Rose's problem is identified by the question: When does freedom lead to irresponsibility? She has a responsibility to her mother and also to her fiancé. How she reconciles this is her internal struggle, a crisis of conscience and also one of courage. This illustrates another aspect of character that we'll now discuss.

CHARACTER STRENGTH AND WEAKNESS

In the *Poetics*, Aristotle talks about what some have come to call the "tragic flaw," a sort of spiritual weakness that eventually does-in the tragic character. It has come down to us this way because of a misreading of the ancient text, but never the less has been found useful in character creation. For a tragic character of heroic proportions, this character flaw will cause his downfall. In the case of the designer of the Titanic, it was arrogance that brought him down. He thought his ship was unsinkable. Character strength and weakness are probably more useful concepts than the "tragic flaw." The weakness may manifest itself as the "underside" of the character, the preacher's weakness for hookers, the movie star's weakness for drugs, or the football player's uncontrollable jealously toward his ex-wife.

Character strength will also come from Premise. This will be the aspect of personality that will get the protagonist into trouble, i.e., put him in conflict with the antagonist. Associated with this strength will also be a weakness. The weakness will be the at-

41

tribute of character that will provide the key to success. Strength gets the character into trouble, and the way he deals with his weakness gets the character out of trouble.

Also, weakness gives the protagonist or antagonist a human quality that will endear him to the reader, particularly if the character has a rather lofty social stature. It makes him seem more human. This weakness may result from the "underside" of the character's strength. A strong desire for independence or liberty can lead to irresponsibility. This irresponsible side will almost cost the character the struggle.

This dual nature of all individuals may well come from the Jungian psychological concepts of the ego and the shadow. We'll discuss them in detail in Chapter 10.

CHARACTER CHANGE

All characters undergo some change during the novel, but the nature of the change for each character will be different. A character who appears in only one scene will experience something that will give him a different perspective. Otherwise your character is a piece of wood. The change in the protagonist will be the most profound.

Types of character change:

- maturational
- intellectual
- emotional
- behavioral (actions)

The change is called the "character arc." The conflict will apply pressure to who he is and result in change. The change will result

Character

in the character either winning or losing the confrontation, or perhaps transcending it. The character who changes gains an edge on his opponent.

CHARACTER ARC

Figure 5 illustrates the change in the protagonist throughout the novel, with the change, and the forces that cause it, broken down. First of all, the essence of the character must be established. This will be followed by that essence being put in jeopardy by identifying a weakness. This will result in the character experiencing the anguish of choice over making a change. The character then struggles to make the change, and this change will be tested at the climax of the story, the three-quarter point, or Second Plot Point. The results, which are demonstrated in the "new" character, are what the entire story is about at the character level.

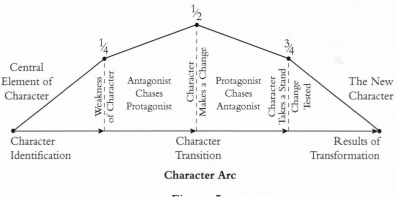

Character Arc

Figure 5

In *Titanic*, both Rose and Jack change. In the beginning, because of her overbearing mother, Rose has accepted a marriage proposal from a man she knows will enslave her. She is on the threshold of suicide. By the end of the movie, she has freed herself from those who would control her and is able to stand on her own. She has found her true self.

Jack is not the same person that he was initially either. In the beginning, he was self-centered, living and traveling Europe on his own with no responsibilities but to pursue his artistic interests, but by the end he has become altruistic. When Jack and Rose are in the freezing ocean water and struggling to stay afloat, they reach a piece of wreckage, but it will only support one of them. Jack puts Rose on it, and then he makes her promise that she will live her life as a free woman. He has transferred his allegiance from himself to Rose, and has given his life to save hers.

On the other hand, Rose's fiancé and her mother do not change internally. They change externally and only increase their opposition to Rose's rebellion. They both want to keep Rose in servitude. They do not struggle internally. This illustrates a central point concerning character. Generally, the character that undergoes the greatest change is the protagonist. This is where the really interesting part of the story lies: the evolution of character.

In Dostoevsky's *Crime and Punishment*, Raskolnikov is the protagonist. He commits murder, is taken into custody and convicted. The second part of the novel is about his punishment in prison where he is rehabilitated through the help of Sonia, a religious prostitute who has fallen in love with him. Raskolnikov is one of the truly great internally tortured characters in literature, along with Shakespeare's Hamlet. Everyone should read these two works to learn the extent to which mental anguish can be exploited.

In the long-running TV series, *Buffy, The Vampire Slayer*, character arc is the single most important reason the series lasted seven years. The characters were constantly growing and changing. Buffy was initially in high school and, in season four, entered college. Her slaying skills, initially rudimentary, became remarkable. During this time, her mother dies, and Buffy has to assume legal responsibility for her sister, Dawn, and their finances. She struggles with becoming fully adult. Willow, Buffy's best friend and a self-taught witch, is initially so timid that she barely recognized her right to exist, but by the end of season six, she almost destroys the world because of her rage at the murder of a loved one.

THE ANGUISH OF CHOICE

As stated in the previous chapter, the Premise contains hidden within it a universal question, particularly if the conflict is internal or involves two rights, i.e., good vs. good instead of good vs. evil. When the protagonist deals with this question, it will be manifested as the "anguish of choice." Answering this question, or the failure to do so, will lead to either victory or defeat. In this way, the story comes down to the character against himself, an internal struggle. In *Hamlet*, the question permeates the entire play in a way it does in few other stories. Hamlet has to take action against his mother, and this leads to the "sublime procrastination" where he even contemplates suicide ("To be or not to be"). Stories in which the protagonist doesn't exhibit the anguish of choice have little, if any, philosophical depth.

The nature of the anguish will be such that it is in essence a search for identity, the recovery of one's self. It's as though the conflict causes the character to discover something about himself that he could not see before. It's a personal blindness. Finding this missing piece of himself will lead to change, and ultimately to victory.

Don't underestimate anguish of choice. Search your story for the moments in which your characters will suffer through it. Find these moments and dramatize them. Don't allow them to happen "off stage" and be described later. This would be a great strategic mistake.

CHARACTER IDENTITY

So far, we have talked about the inside of character. The external part of character concerns the persona, what he projects to the outside world. This is the social façade, the mask. This is the "pollen" that has or will collect around the "heart" of the character. The central questions about character creation are: Is the person identifiable? Does he have an identity? What characteristics distinguish him from every other person on the planet?

Any method the author uses that answers these questions will probably work, provided the character has a proper relationship with the storyline. Characters exist only within the story, and generally, should have no attributes unrelated to it. The characters that populate a novel are not as broad as real-life people. This does not mean that they should be stereotypes or stick figures. For example, a complete psychoanalysis of the antagonist might be okay in a story about a serial killer, but might be inappropriate for the main character in a traditional western.

Character identity is more readily discovered than created. You can build his background, a biography for your character, but unless it fits with your original concept of the story, he just won't work. You can't arbitrarily make up facts about a character and then shoe-horn him into the story.

Another effective way of developing character is through what other characters say about him. Occasionally a main character will not even appear in the novel, and sometimes what the author leaves out about the main character can be telling. In Daphne du Maurier's *Rebecca*, not only does Rebecca not appear in the novel (she's dead) but the story's protagonist, the new Mrs. DeWinter, is never given a name. She has little identity outside that as her husband's wife. This has been so skillfully executed by the author that the reader rarely realizes it unless told. This has the effect of bringing Rebecca, the missing character, to the forefront and increasing her influence on the entire work.

The character's identity should exist on many levels. He should be identifiable physically, have a distinctive voice, distinctive actions, emotions, motives, and social status. The point-of-view character (discussed in Chapter 4) must be identifiable internally: the way he thinks, worries, and deals with himself. We will also be able to see into the minds of other characters, but always indirectly.

In ancient Greece, when an actor played a part, he donned a mask, the mask of Dionysus. Dionysus is the patron god of theatre and the god of the mask. Within the domain of Dionysus, illusion exists simultaneously with reality. The mask represents the persona, the illusion of the character, and the author must symbolically don the mask of each of his characters in tern as he writes.

PSYCHOLOGY

Before we get into building a character, let's delve into a little psychology. Psychology is kept separate for a reason: psychobabble can destroy a good novel. Still yet, understanding a little psychology can help add depth to a character. Just be careful that you don't deconstruct the character by using too much narrative insight.

Character

During decades of work as a therapist, Carl Jung developed an extensive theory of personality types. His work, titled simply *Psychological Types*, is a classic in the field. Jung identified four pairs of preferences: extraversion/introversion, sensation/intuition, thinking/feeling, and perceiving/judging. His theory is that every person has a particular mix, and emphasis, of these preferences. A simple, practical application of Jung's work in this area is contained in *Please Understand Me, Character & Temperament Types* by David Keirsey and Marilyn Bates. This book uses the Myers-Briggs Type Indicator test as a tool for identifying sixteen different patterns of personality. Even more interesting is that the authors relate these personality types to the professions and interests of individuals. Not everyone is a big fan of this approach to an individual's psychology, but you as an author don't have to be a disciple to use this tool for fleshing out a character. I've taken the test myself and found it to be amazingly accurate.

Keirsey and Bates also tell us that opposite personality types frequently attract, so that you can gain considerable insight into the secondary characters that your protagonist will bring into his life, and the origin of any conflicts that exists between them. You might consider having each of the characters take the type test. As an example of opposites, one might envision a rather dimwitted man who is attracted to a smart woman. Although he might be attracted to her intellect, he could also feel threatened by her superiority. If these two really care about each other, the good-natured banter between them would enliven the relationship. He might be better at controlling the spending, even though she'd have to balance the checkbook. The possibilities are endless, and these aspects of character don't just apply to the protagonist and antagonist, but also to the characters involved in the subplots.

Character

Another aspect of character psychology concerns the stages of life we all experience. Books have been written on the subject, the most popular of which, published several years ago, is aptly titled *Passages*, and was written by Gail Sheehy. Another excellent book is Murray Stein's *In Midlife*, which uses the myth of Odysseus' ten-year odyssey about the Aegean to provide insight into the underlying forces driving the mid-life crisis. This book is also a useful introduction to the relatively new and fascinating field of archetypal psychology.

The way a character presents himself to the world, along with his inherited attributes, speaks volumes about what goes on inside him. A man who combs his hair over his bald spot has a certain insecurity about his appearance. A woman who won't quit talking is protecting herself from her audience. Some experts will advise you to provide each of your characters with a "tic," some persistent trait of character or behavior. This gives the author something to describe each time the character comes on the scene and makes the character immediately identifiable to the reader. In Fitzgerald's *The Great Gatsby*, Gatsby calls Nick "old sport." This is an affectation that Gatsby assumed to convince people he was an Oxford graduate. The tic fit Gatsby perfectly, because it was part of his false front. This may be a good idea generally, but don't think that, once you've invented a tic, you've solved the characterization problem. This tic must fit with the character's basic nature, and the character must be fully developed in other ways. But it is at least a place to start with your character's mannerisms, and it's something to which you can add as you proceed.

As another example, in the movie *When Harry Met Sally*, Sally had the really irritating habit of giving lengthy instructions to waiters in restaurants. This gave Harry something to play off of, and eventually, he came to find this trying aspect of her personality endearing.

PHYSICAL APPEARANCE

To develop the way a character presents his physical self to the world, you don't have to tolerate plausibility as an obstacle. Take this example from a recently published novel by Hilary Mantel titled *Beyond Black*:

> Alison was a woman who seemed to fill a room, even when she wasn't in it. She was of an unfeasible size, with plump creamy shoulders, rounded calves, thighs and hips that overflowed her chair; she was soft as an Edwardian, opulent as a showgirl, and when she moved you could hear (though she did not wear them) the rustle of plumes and silks. In a small space, she seemed to use up more than her share of the oxygen; in return her skin breathed out moist perfumes, like a giant tropical flower. When you came into a room she'd left--her bedroom, her hotel room, her dressing room backstage--you felt her as a presence, a trail. Alison had gone, but you would see a chemical mist of hair spray falling through the bright air. On the floor would be a line of talcum powder, and her scent--*Je Reviens*--would linger in curtain fabric, in cushions, and in the weave of towels. When she headed for a spirit encounter, her path was charged, electric; when her body was out on stage, her face--cheeks glowing, eyes alight--seemed to float still in the dressing room mirror.[17]

Note the mixture of concrete physical attributes gradually progressing to the more subjective—as if this was the way that people viewed her—to the clearly untrue and even esoteric. But this woman is a medium, and she projects her profession with her presence and even her absence.

CHARACTER VOICE

Voice, the way a character speaks, will reveal many things about him: education, social class, mood, and intelligence. Hence, all dialogue carries the indelible style of the character in the same way a fingerprint is unique; therefore, dialogue also distinguishes between characters. Dialogue can't be written the way people speak, but is presented in edited form. It must be "portrayed." Voice can be viewed as the author's act of impersonating the character. The author takes dictation, but it is a strange sort of dictation. Dialogue is a distillation of real life conversation, not a transcription, and frequently only expresses an emotion about the subject, not necessarily factual content.

CHARACTER ACTION: Speaking without words.

What a character does will always speak louder than what the narrator says about him. You can say your character is in an uncontrollable rage, but if the character punches someone in the mouth, you get your point across better. One character may resort to violence to resolve a conflict, whereas another may become subdued, and hide within himself.

Body language is different than other types of action. Body language is the way a person uses his body that unconsciously signals his emotional state. For example, when seated, some people cross their arms or legs when they feel threatened in a conversation. The author should go into a coffee shop and watch the clientele, the way they posture themselves around their friends, and how their actions change when a stranger approaches. Watch the people behind the counter, how they physical change from customer to customer. Learn to detect the ebb and flow of human emotion, signaled by body language.

CHARACTER EMOTION: The pulse of passion.

The degree to which the reader feels the character's emotions is the degree to which he will believe the character's actions. Do not tell what the characters are feeling; allow them to express it. Be skeptical of any rules dictating how a character must act. "Experts" frequently say that characters must be passionate and take a definite, single-minded stance in the conflict. One of the most memorable characters, Hamlet, couldn't make up his mind about anything. Don't destroy your characters' originality. In Anne Tyler's *The Accidental Tourist* (which was made into a successful movie), the main character wasn't passionate about anything and lived in a miasma of self-doubt.

Once again, when exposing a character's psychology don't resort to psychobabble. You don't need to be a psychiatrist to write good characters. If you trust your characters, and understand their passions, they will show you how they act through their own impulses. Writing characters is fun and exciting. Go on the adventure with them. The more you become surprised by your characters' actions, the less you have to worry about technique. Let them lead you into unknown territory.

CHARACTER MOTIVATION

Characters should have their own motivations and not be subject to the will of the author. The author doesn't put motivations into the characters but pulls motivations important to the story from within the character. The reader can always tell the source of motivations, and if they don't come from within the character, the reader will detect it immediately. A good check to ensure that each character becomes real is to ask if each has his own agenda, and whether it shows in his dialogue and actions. They should never simply fulfill the author's intentions. To accomplish this, the author must "launder" all his intentions toward the storyline through his characters (much as the mob launders drug money through false bank accounts).

CHARACTER SOCIAL STATUS

In addition to pure social class (aristocrat, peasant), profession (king, queen, engineer, mother, commander-in-chief, hobo) will also play a part. In American novels, social class tends to be less important than the section of the country he comes from and his ethnic origin. Working-class Americans constitute the most of us, but we do increasing encounter the very wealthy and the very poor. Political affiliation is becoming increasingly important.

CHARACTER THOUGHTS

Explicit character thoughts will generally be limited to the point of view character, and in a first-person narration, exclusively those of the narrator. The way people think is different from the way they speak. Their thoughts may reveal a kinder side of themselves that they are afraid to show the world, or an underbelly that is too provocative, corrupt, or violent to let see the light of day. In any case, thoughts will expose another level of character and divulge internal struggles.

Character

SUMMARY

As shown in Figure 6, the author funnels all these character-istics into a single character to form his identity, and performs the same activity for each character.

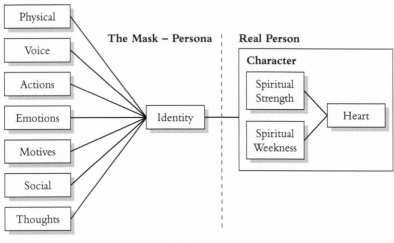

Figure 6

The author should also know things about the character that are not included. Writing a character biography can be helpful, but select only details that play an important part in the story. Approach your characters obliquely, possibly not even as human beings. You might consider describing them as though they are a piece of mechanical equipment, a tree, or an animal. Homer, in *The Iliad*, describes Agamemnon, the commanding general of the Greek forces at Troy, this way:

Agamemnon's lordly mien
was like the mien of Zeus whose joy is lightning;

Character

oaken-waisted as Ares, god of war,
he seemed, and deep-chested as Lord Poseidon;
and, as a great bull in his majesty
towers supreme amid a grazing herd...[18]

We get the picture of him as lion, oak tree, and bull as he is compared to three Greek gods, all of which makes him seem formidable, and ironically, more human. In another description, that from Euripides in his play, *Iphigeneia at Aulis*, Agamemnon is presented differently. Agamemnon's brother reminds Agamemnon of how he came to be commander:

> ...do you remember how humble you were, clasping every man's hand, keeping your door unlocked to any commoner who wished to enter, and opening yourself to conversation with all and sundry even when they didn't seek it? You sought by your demeanor to buy advancement from the multitude. Then when you had won office, you changed your manner and were no longer as friendly to your former friends as before: you were hard to approach and kept yourself scarce within doors. The good man ought not to change his character when he fares well.[19]

Agamemnon now seems approachable. He's two-faced. He's further described as uncertain, even cowardly, when it comes time for him to sacrifice his daughter to gain favorable winds from the gods to sail to Troy. Agamemnon is a character in crisis.

A character can, and should, have weaknesses, but when the author discredits a character, even a bad guy, he discredits the novel. All characters should have a center of integrity. Agamemnon acts "cowardly" toward sacrificing Iphigenia because he loves her, and because he is a caring father. Thus, he retains his integrity while also exposing his ruthless nature and craving for power. It also illustrates anguish of choice.

TYPES OF CHARACTERS

We've already discussed the protagonist and antagonist. Other types of characters frequently populate novels, and you would do well to realize who they are, since it might help flesh-out the character. Some of the more prevalent character types are discussed below, although the list is far from complete.

a. The Thematic Character

The thematic character conveys special knowledge to the protagonist that gives him an advantage in the conflict. The number of times that a thematic character shows up in a story is absolutely amazing. He is never the protagonist nor the antagonist, but generally has a close relationship with the protagonist. The thematic character will probably be the third most important character after the protagonist and antagonist. His special knowledge is inherently a part of the Premise and is closely related to the nature of the conflict. Thematic characters are historically some of the most interesting ever created and, in many cases, irresistible to readers. They satisfy a basic need in story telling, and probably in the human psyche: a need for wisdom.

Obi-Wan Kenobi is the thematic character in *Star Wars*. He teaches Luke about the Force, the good and bad of it, which enables Luke to overcome the evil forces of Darth Vader. In the movie *Titanic,* Jack is the thematic character; he teaches Rose about freedom and warns her of the consequences of social bondage. In the more recent TV series *Buffy, The Vampire Slayer*, the thematic character is her Watcher, Giles, an Englishman, who comes to the States specifically to advise and train Buffy in the ancient art of vampire slaying. In Tolkien's *The Lord of the Rings*, the thematic character is Gandalf. As an immortal wizard, who has lived in Middle-earth for thousands of years, he provides guidance not only to the Hobbits but to all those involved in the war against the evil forces of Sauron.

b. Groups as Characters

Characters don't have to be individual human beings. They can be families, as in *Romeo and Juliet*, where the Montagues and the Capulets are feuding and the lovers are caught in the conflict that destroys them; or countries, as in *The Hunt for Red October*, where the USA and the USSR are in conflict over the desperate search for a rogue nuclear submarine. In this type of story in which larger social forces determine many of the events, these countries as "characters" are treated psychologically as though they are people. Countries exhibit human characteristics: arrogance, anger, jealousy, etc. They will also have an arc.

In short, any social unit can serve as a character and should be structurally treated as such in a novel.

c. Peripheral Characters and Subplots.

Now that we understand how characters relate to the novel, we can start to understand secondary characters and subplots. Subplots have all the characteristics of the main plot, although they may not be a part of the full novel from beginning to end. They have a setup, 1st plot point, mid-course reversal, etc. Each subplot is associated with a secondary character. The subplot conflict will be locked with the entrance of the character. All the subplots will be closely associated with the main storyline. A Premise may be written for each peripheral character involved in a subplot. This Premise will help identify the heart of the character, thus allowing him to become well-rounded within the story. The author can identify the arc associated with each and draw a geometric subplot diagram, just as he has done with the main plot.

In *Titanic*, the conflict between Jack and Cal (Rose's fiancé) is a subplot resolved when Rose helps Jack escape from being handcuffed inside the sinking Titanic.

d. Characters Within a Larger Social Context.

In *Titanic*, the love story between Rose and Jack is played out against the larger story of the sinking of the Titanic. In Boris Pasternak's *Doctor Zhivago*, we witness the lives of highly developed characters played out against the First World War and the Russian revolution. We also see this type of story in *The Hunt for Red October*, where we have minimal characterization in a story about an international incident involving a nuclear submarine. Other stories of this nature are Carl Sagan's sci-fi novel, *Contact*, and a host of volcano-eruption and asteroid-impact movies. What is crucial in this type of story is that the Premise be reflected in both aspects of the storyline, i.e., the conflict involving the characters must be linked with the larger social conflict. In *Doctor Zhivago*, the main character is a "confessional" poet, a man very much involved in the "personal." The revolution is about the death of personal life in Russia in favor of a communal life dictated by the state.

REDEMPTION

Guided by Premise, the author must decide the ultimate fate

of his characters. Depending on the type of novel you're writing and the Premise, each of your characters will meet his appropriate fate. Some will be redeemed on a spiritual level, while others will be left to wallow in their own pettiness. The one who learns from the conflict transcends it and will be redeemed. This constitutes the end of the story.

★

Of course, many stories (novels and movies) are successful and yet don't satisfy all the character requirements set forth here. Although other examples certainly exist, many adventure stories fall into this category. The success of these stories is generally due to a charismatic hero who captures the reader's imagination. Our interest in the hero is peaked by his extraordinary abilities rather than character growth through anguish of choice. Spielberg's Indiana Jones doesn't have many moments of profound, personal decision-making. It is his strength, endurance, fighting ability, and that uncanny knack for getting out of trouble that we admire and keeps us returning for each sequel. These movies succeed because of a larger-than-life hero. But these stories don't cause us to reflect on who we are or necessarily help us mature as human beings. They may, however, send us into the mountains or to a foreign country seeking adventure.

CHARACTER BONDING

A word of caution about conflict. Conflict is so central to providing story progression and a sense of realism that it must exist even between friends. Human interaction is extremely complex, and any scene that doesn't have an element of conflict will be flat. However, in recent years there has been a tendency to create sharp, destructive conflict between characters in what would ordinarily be a friendly relationship. Some authors will even say that conflict is the only thing of interest in fiction. This is simply not true. As a matter of fact, bonding between friends is often essential to providing sympathetic, meaningful characters, and is sometimes even central to the story. The moments when they come together to comfort each other can be profound.

Two examples of this that have captured the public's imagination in recent years are J. K. Rowling's *Harry Potter* series, and J. R. R. Tolkien's *The Lord of the Rings*. Harry Potter without Ron Weasley and Hermione Granger would be dull, if not unimaginable. These three characters, though they do argue, are very close and care for each other deeply. This is also true of the Hobbits in Tolkien's novel. Frodo, Sam, Merry and Pippin form a tight-knit group, deeply committed to each other. Authors should not be overly conscious of creating conflict at the expense of friendship.

Another example is Joss Whedon's TV series *Buffy, The Vampire Slayer*. Fans of the series are addicted to the interaction between Buffy and her friends and family. In several episodes, friendship has been brought to the forefront as reinforcement; one of the primary reasons Buffy is such a good slayer, and has lived longer than most, is her ability to make and use friends to help her stave off the forces of evil. Slayers don't generally live long lives.

Yet, stories of the loner action hero are also plentiful. The loner that Clint Eastwood played in some of his earlier films, for example *High Planes Drifter,* had this quality. We know nothing of his family or friends, his past or what he wants in the future. We don't even know his name. All this lack of information adds an atmosphere of mystery and a sense of mysticism.

The main point here is to be true to the vision of your characters and story and not rely too heavily on what self-proclaimed

Character

experts call "the rules." Be a renegade. Write about the special
bonds between characters. Write something no one has seen before. Just be good at it.

ONE PARAGRAPH SUMMARY
    Character and plot are inseparable. The central plot is defined
by the conflict between opposing wills, those of the main characters as defined in the Premise. Each of the storyline milestones
will test or stress the main character in a new way. This will force
a reconsideration of who he is. Characters drive the storyline. The
protagonist, antagonist, and thematic character are not just connected to the story: they are the story. Character wishes and fears,
along with his resulting decisions, constantly propel the story into
the future. Ideas and emotion determine character motivation.
Emotion may drive the character in a direction he doesn't agree
with intellectually, creating internal conflict.

EXERCISES
(a) Provide a character sketch for each primary character, stating
the "heart" or central aspect of each along with their strength and
weakness. (b) Draw and label the arc diagram for each character
to demonstrate how they change. (c) For secondary characters,
and perhaps even those that only momentarily enter the story
and never return, consider how that momentary encounter might
have an impact and in some way change the secondary character.

CHAPTER 4: Narration

Who will spin this splendid illusion of reality, this thing called a novel? The narrator is the one who tells the story. Narration is the most complex element of fiction since it defines the relationship between the reader and the story. The most important decision the novelsmith makes regards the type of narration best suited to his novel. Narration is everything, literally every word on the page.

The structure of a novel, as described in Chapter 1, is like the framework of a great building. The entire story rests on the framework, but it is never seen. What is "seen" is the narration. This is where the actual story gets told and equates to the outward appearance of the building: the texture of the walls, the carpet, the lighting and furnishings. Everything within, that with which the reader comes into contact, occurs in the narration. Just as the reader depends on a character to reveal the human impact of the story, the reader also depends entirely on seeing the story through the narrative eye.

The narrator not only tells the story, he does it with style. Style is everything in narration. If a place exists where craft and art are inseparable, it's in narration. Narrative style may give the novel integrity and perhaps add a little pizzazz, or conversely make it a nondescript jumble of boring words unworthy of the light of day.

Narration

Style is primarily a matter of voice, how the narrator "speaks" to the reader; and voice, for the author, is a matter of being spoken to from within. The author taps into the narrative voice within himself, sometimes to the extent that it seems to the author that he is channeling someone external to himself. A narrator must be a little touched by "madness." Intelligence and ingenuity shine here like nowhere else. The novelist is somewhat of a poet, and the weaving of ideas with images and metaphor is what makes the ingredients a soup and the reader a willing consumer. The narrator must sweeten the reader's palate.

To accomplish the illusion, someone must tell the story. In times past, the illusionist was frequently the author. But authors have, through the years, gradually divorced themselves from their own work by bringing someone else in to tell the story. This is particularly so in the American novel. Statements like the following rarely if ever show up any more:

> This is what I undertake to do for you, reader. With this drop of ink at the end of my pen, I will show you...[20]

Note the way the author pulls the reader into his confidence, and even shows him the act of putting the words on the page. In this way, the author forms a bond with the reader that persists throughout the work.

The modern author will step back from the narration to a point where another character is born: the narrator. This new character will then tell the entire story and is, in fact, the author's surrogate. The degree to which the narrator becomes a personage in the story varies widely. Some stories are told in first person, and in this technique, the narrator will actually be one of the characters, frequently the main character. In other novels, the identity of the narrator will be so nebulous that it seems to be the author but is, in fact, an entity separate from and not the author. This style of narration, however, wasn't invented yesterday. *Moby Dick*, published in 1851, starts with the words, "Call me Ishmael," and the reader realizes immediately that Melville himself has stepped into the background and is letting someone else tell the story of the great white whale.

Yet, some remnants of the author as narrator still remain. For example, consider Richard Bach's *Illusions*. The character telling the story is named Richard, and the author intends the reader to assume that this "Richard" is the author. But the story contains appearing-and-disappearing vampires and episodes of walking on water, so that the reader realizes a good deal of artistic license is at work. Many readers love this stuff because it gives an intense sense of reality while opening up a mystical world full of new possibilities. Robert James Waller in *The Bridges of Madison County* handled this type of narrative sleight-of-hand so skillfully, that millions of readers naïvely assumed that a principal character, a photographer, had actually written an article for *National Geographic*. The magazine received many calls from readers enquiring about the non-existent article. This is a marvelous example of the author conning the reader into suspending disbelief, a subject that will be covered extensively later in this chapter.

The narrator can be practically anyone or any thing: woman or man, a child, someone long dead, or perhaps even an animal. Ursula K. LeGuin tells her short story, *The Wife's Story*, through the eyes of a she-wolf. What is crucial is that the author realize that he must craft a narrator. This may seem obvious, but a beginning novelist will frequently underestimate its importance. Rarely will the novice dedicate anywhere near as much time to inventing the narrator as he will to inventing a character. Not only is the "identity" of the narrator important, but the narrator's methods of storytelling are, in some genres, highly developed and rigidly controlled. The narration will be the first thing noticed by the potential agent or publisher and is the place to show that you know your craft.

The author's job is to create a narrator to match the story. The relationship between author, narrator and story is pictorially represented in Figure 7:

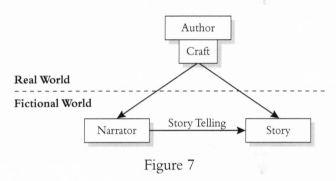

Figure 7

Notice that the author creates the narrator through craft and that the narrator resides in the fictional world. Again, the narrator is the author's surrogate, and the author does not tell the story. The author should keep this in mind throughout the planning of the novel because the limitations placed on the narrator, depending on the narrative technique, determine much of the novel's structure. That's why, even though the beginning novelsmith may have a great story, he may still fail to produce a publishable novel. Alternatively, many weak stories have been published and sold well simply because of an appealing narrative voice.

Narration

You might well ask: What then is the situation of the author relative to his own work? And the answer is that the author is the craftsman and practices his trade as a novelsmith. But the author is also the first reader of the work, and as a craftsman, the author tries to read the work-in-progress as a reader, so that he might gain some perspective on it. As the author writes the novel, continuing to accumulate paragraph after paragraph, a transformation gradually takes place. At first, the inspiration for the novel is contained exclusively in the author's own head, but as time goes by, as he gets the story on paper, the author gradually becomes more and more a reader of his own story. This transformation process is illustrated in Figure 8:

Author Transformation

Figure 8

This transformation from craftsman to reader must take place for the author to eventually consider the novel finished, and is, therefore, critical relative to the later stages of editing. As the novel becomes more and more complete, the author allows himself to get more involved in the story and reads with more and more suspension of disbelief, thus gradually becoming just another reader of his own work. This is also a complex process to be discussed in greater detail in Chapter 12.

CREATING THE NARRATOR

To craft the narration correctly, we must study the nature of the relationship between the narrator, who will create the fictional dream, and the reader. This relationship is illustrated in Figure 9:

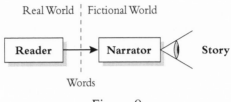

Figure 9

Note that the narrator exists in the fictional world and the reader in the real world. Only words fill the gap. The narrator always stands between the story and the reader; consequently, any deviation by the author from his chosen narrative stance shocks the reader. The author must understand the complexity of narration, so he can provide the reader with a consistent, coherent narrative.

POINT OF VIEW

Point of view (POV) is the answer to the question of vantage point: Who stands where to watch the action? In movie making, this is determined by the director: Where to place the camera? Determining POV is the most important decision the author will make concerning novel structure, and it must be decided early to avoid disaster. The narrator views and tells the entire story, and deciding the narrative POV will affect how the reader responds to the novel emotionally and morally. The place to go to determine what POV to use is, of course, the Premise. The way the author wants the reader to view the Premise will determine POV.

To determine POV, the question most often asked is: Whose story is it? Generally, this will be the protagonist, as identified in the Premise, but it doesn't have to be. In Fitzgerald's *The Great Gatsby* (a story of a bootlegger who tries to steal a man's wife right from under his nose) the story is narrated by a peripheral, rather bland character named Nick, a cousin of the wife. Fitzgerald's choice of narrator has produced a rather interesting literary discussion concerning whose story he is really telling: Gatsby's or Nick's? In most cases, though the story will belong to the protagonist, leaving the author to decide whether to let the character himself tell the story or provide a third-person narrator.

In Flaubert's third-person narration, *Madam Bovary*, with Emma Bovary as the POV character, we feel her frustration, sexual passion, her guilt, and shame. We empathize with her, because we experience the trail of events as she does and experience her desire, her passion. But our sympathies would be considerably different if the story were told from her husband's POV. Narrative closeness generally creates empathy because we can "see" a character's motives and feel what he feels. If Flaubert had told the story from the husband's POV, we'd feel his jealousy and anger. Since we see the story from Emma's POV, we empathize with her, even though, from an objective perspective, she's a louse.

Restricting the POV to that of a single character also provides more intensity and immediacy. This may not be obvious, and the reasons for it are rather obscure, but it's probably because the reader becomes centered within a character and learns to interpret the world through him. Remember, the reader is piggybacked on the POV character. This is the way we experience the real world, seeing everything from our own perspective. The reader's transference of experience to another character, who exists in a world where the reader does not, is natural. A change in POV destroys this affinity, which, when left alone, deepens as the reader gets further into the story.

Inconsistency with POV appears amateurish. Although multiple POVs can be used to good effect, breaks in POV generally should not occur. Beginning writers seem to take their queue from movies in which POV is less tightly controlled and shifts occur frequently. One thing is certain: learning to use POV correctly is as important for novel writing as is writing a good sentence.

Henry James perfected the restricted third-person POV and felt that omniscience was an irresponsible way of writing fiction. But the omniscient POV has its place, and some will argue that it is the best approach. J. R. R. Tolkien used omniscience for his sprawling and many charactered, enormously successful, fantasy novel, *The Lord of the Rings*. The only advice I can give is to understand POV, its impact on the reader, and how a break in it disorients the reader. To misunderstand its use spells catastrophe. Writers who don't understand POV write sloppy novels.

One obvious situation where an omniscient narrator can be used to good effect is in a story about an event, such as in Tom Clancy's *Red Storm Rising*. In this novel, the narrator jumps all over the globe, first to Siberia, then California, then Washington DC. Different characters populate the setting at each location. Clancy gets away with it because his novel is about a military conflict between the Soviet Union and the United States. It's about that event, and the people only play a supporting role. Actually, the novel's main characters are the two countries. The novel suffers somewhat because Clancy never really settles on a human character with whom the reader can identify, and the emotional intensity of the story never quite rings true. Still, the novel was a bestseller, and he achieved a marvelous portrayal of international tension with the continual continent-jumping.

Narration

FIRST PERSON

In first-person narration, a character (I went…) tells the story. To stay true to the POV, the narrator then has no access to another character's thoughts unless told them directly and, therefore, can only provide what the POV character would know. One of the most famous first-person novels of all time is Melville's *Moby Dick*. Melville opens the novel this way:

> Call me Ishmael. Some years ago—never mind how long precisely—having little or no money in my purse, and nothing particular to interest me on shore, I thought I would sail about a little and see the watery part of the world.[21]

We are in the hands of Ishmael for the entire novel without a break in POV. In other first-person novels, we might be in the hands of one character for a chapter or two and then be passed off to another character for a look at the story from a different POV.

Dostoevsky originally wrote the first chapters of *Crime and Punishment* using first-person narration (once as a confessional, the other as a diary), then realized that this POV was a mistake, cast all he had done overboard, and rewrote it in third person.[22] In this psychological novel, the protagonist (a murderer) might not have been sympathetic enough for the reader to feel comfortable residing in his head. The substitution of an "outside," third-person narrator with access to the character's thoughts provided the necessary esthetic distance for the reader's comfort. Dostoevsky agonized over this POV decision for some time. His process is instructive and has been documented in Joseph Frank's biography of Dostoevsky. The beginning novelsmith, and the experienced one for that matter, would do well to read Frank's description of Dostoevsky's decision-making process.

Another interesting novel is Barbara Kingsolver's *Animal Dreams*. This first-person narrative about a young woman contains isolated, short, two-to-three page chapters written in third person from her father's POV. Her father suffers from Alzheimer's, and these short chapters are the most powerful in the novel.

SECOND PERSON

In second-person narration (You went...) either: (a) the narrator tells the story to another character, or (b) the narrator speaks to the reader as if the reader is a character in the story. Here's the opening in one of the all-time best selling "second-person" novels:

> You are not the kind of guy who would be at a place like this at this time of the morning. But here you are, and you cannot say that the terrain is entirely unfamiliar, although the details are fuzzy. You are in a nightclub talking to a girl with a shaved head.[23]

The novel was made into a movie, but much of the story's charm came from the second-person narration and was lost in translation to the big screen. The movie, which starred Michael J. Fox, was not much of a success at the box office.

THIRD PERSON

Third-person narration (She went...) takes on many forms. The narrator is somewhat divorced from the story and may even be totally omniscient. The omniscient narrator is able to see the story from anyone's perspective and to "hear" the thoughts of all the characters. The unrestricted omniscient narrator is little used in the modern American novel, except in poorly-written pop fiction. The modern novel tends to limit the narration to the perspective of one person and to only have access to that person's thoughts. This POV is called "limited omniscient." With this perspective, the narrator can tell about anything the POV character can see, hear or know about, but can describe events that occur "across town," so to speak, only if told by another character.

NARRATIVE VOICE

One of the strongest narrative voices in all literature comes from the autobiography of a seven-year-old girl. It starts out like this:

> Today the folks are gone away from the house we do live in. They are gone a little way away, to the ranch house where the grandpa does live. I sit on our step, and I do print. I like it, this house we do live in, being at the edge of the near woods. So many little people do live in the near woods. I do have conversations with them. I found a near woods first day I did go explores. That was the next day after we were come here.[24]

Though this isn't an artifice of some author's grand purpose (Opal was really seven years old when she wrote this), it does demonstrate the distinctiveness provided by voice and its attraction for the reader.

Homer started *The Odyssey* this way:

Sing in me, Muse, and through me tell the story

of that man skilled in all ways of contending,
the wanderer, harried for years on end,
after he plundered the stronghold
on the proud height of Troy.[25]

Homer's narrative has a lofted, singing quality, one that comes from the fact that he wrote from an oral tradition in which the stories, as epic poetry, were actually sung.

Narrative voice is the way the story "sounds." It sets tone, tension, time period, and much more. When captured properly, the narrative voice ringing true is enough for the novelsmith to do his work, even if he knows little else about craft. It can solve many writing problems because everything comes through it. All the author has to do is listen to the Muse. In this way, the author's intuition about storytelling is enough to pull him through.

AUTHORIAL DISTANCE

The author should strive to remove himself from his own novel by laundering his motivations through the characters. Author intentions superimposed on the story result in contrived plots. Allow your characters to force the action instead of allowing your intentions, as author, to filter through. View your own intentions as drug money that must be laundered through your characters.

You, as the author, are not a part of the fictional world and must remain outside it. The third-person narrator, though a part of the fictional world, is still not a part of the story and must stay out of it also. The first-person narrator is a part of the story and his motivations may play a part in it.

Narration

THE BACKSTORY

Jump into the story. Avoid flashbacks. You lose the reader's interest when the narrator drifts from the storyline. A flashback works best when the reader has been prepared for a previous event to the point where the information is really important to him. If you have a character with epilepsy, instead of telling the history of the illness, tell of its origin when the first seizure occurs, or when the character first worries about an impending attack. Don't tell the story of the illness in the beginning simply because you know the reader will need the information later.

In Ron Hansen's *Mariette in Ecstasy*, a young postulant enters a convent where, twenty years before, her older sister also became a nun. During the first meeting between the two at the convent, the narrator provides the following information about Mariette's sister, Mother Céline the prioress:

> Mother Céline seems a glamorous actress playing a nun, or one of the grand ladies of inheritance that Mariette has seen in paintings of English society. Without her black veil and gray habit, the prioress would seem a genteel and handsome mother of less than forty, blond and lithe and Continental, but tense and initiating, too, with green eyes that seem to strike what they see. She was Annette Baptiste and a junior at Vassar when Mariette was born, Sister Céline and a novice when their mother died, the prioress of Our Lady of Sorrows since Mariette was twelve. She arranges and grooms her papers on the green felt of the desktop and then she briskly sits opposite Mariette and puts her hands on her knees as she asks, "Are you happy?"[26]

Narration

Tucked away in the third sentence of this paragraph is a summary of the relationship between the two sisters, and even the added fact that their mother is dead, all within the sister's short, one-sentence biography. This method provides the backstory without interruption to the narrative flow, and provides the reader with the necessary information when it's needed. The reader is probably unconscious of the author's sleight of hand. A few sentences like this sprinkled throughout a novel can add to the reader's enjoyment rather than distract the reader from the flow of the story.

The big accomplishment of this technique is to free up the author to start the novel at the time when the central conflict is locked as opposed to providing all the background material in a prior chapter. The reader will be pulled into the story by the conflict and propelled along to its resolution.

TENSE: PAST, PRESENT OR FUTURE?

The main stream of the storyline is generally told in a single tense although deviations from a central tense may occur temporarily to provide a more distinctive flashback narrative or during some other such narrative discontinuity. In Dennis McFarland's *The Music Room*, the main storyline is written in past tense with flashbacks, ironically, in present tense, an approach that works beautifully.

PRESENT TENSE

In present-tense narration, the action happens as the narrator speaks (She goes...). Sometimes an author will even employ present perfect tense (She is going...). Present tense has a quality of discovery about it and can give the story more of a sense of immediacy. But its shortcoming is that the narrator doesn't know what is to happen next and can have little if any perspective on events. The narrator can't give that philosophic quality which comes from looking back on a story. Consider this passage from a present-tense novel:

> I can see by my watch, without taking my hand from the left grip of the cycle, that it is eight-thirty in the morning. The wind, even at sixty miles an hour, is warm and humid. When it's this hot and muggy at eight-thirty, I'm wondering what it's going to be like in the afternoon.
>
> In the wind are pungent odors from the marshes by the road. We are in an area of the Central Plains filled with thousands of duck hunting sloughs, heading northwest from Minneapolis toward the Dakotas. This highway is an old concrete two-laner that hasn't had much traffic since a four-laner went in parallel to it several years ago. When we pass a marsh the air suddenly becomes cooler. Then, when we are past, it suddenly warms up again.[27]

Note how well the present-tense narrative combines with the sensory information ("warm and humid," "pungent odors") to heighten the sense of immediacy, place the reader firmly in the setting, and make him emotionally responsive to the action.

PAST TENSE

In past-tense narration, the action has taken place sometime in the past (She went...). The narrator has an overview of the complete story and can construct a narrative with the perspective of a historian. It can have a quality of continual foreshadowing. Consider this famous opening:

Narration

It was the best of times, it was the worst of times, it was the age of wisdom, it was the age of foolishness, it was the epoch of belief, it was the epoch of incredulity, it was the season of Light, it was the season of Darkness, it was the spring of hope, it was the winter of despair, we had everything before us, we had nothing before us, we were all going direct to Heaven, we were all going the other way—in short, the period was so far like the present period, that some of its noisiest authorities insisted on its being received, for good or evil, in the superlative degree of comparison only.[28]

The novel was set seventy-five years in the past. This gave Dickens' narrator the perspective to evaluate and characterize the time period in his opening paragraph, something no one alive at the time in which the novel was set could have done.

CREATING STORY

Sense of story comes from narrative technique. "Story" is the inevitable forward momentum of events, originating in conflict and driven by cause and effect to a resolution. Anticipation is the reader's sense of inevitable forward motion caused by the developing conflict. Story, therefore, has its birth in Premise. Once the conflict is locked, the characters will develop expectations and a sense of purpose. Their wishes and decisions will constantly propel them into the future. In addition, they will be swept up in the current of life around them. The world should also not be static, but dynamic, the events reinforcing the main theme, the Premise, of the work. In *Titanic*, the characters are greatly affected by the sinking of the great ship. The event, over which they have no control, forces them to make Premise-related decisions that affect their lives.

Of Homer's two epic poems, *The Odyssey* tends to be more episodic (except toward the end when Odysseus arrives home and confronts Penelope's suitors) and *The Iliad* more plot-driven. Odysseus' encounters with the Cyclopes and the goddess Circe occur because he washes up on their shores, and not because of some plot requirement to see those characters. These loosely connected episodes are not tightly plotted events. However, each episode is internally plotted because each involves a conflict. The overarching element in *The Odyssey* is Odysseus' conflict with the god Poseidon and his desire to return home. In *The Iliad*, Homer opens the story with a conflict between Agamemnon, commander of the Greek army, and Achilles, the Greek's most powerful warrior. This personal conflict then plays out against the war with Troy. And even the Trojan War plays out against the cosmic conflict between two factions within the Olympian gods.

SUSPENSE

Suspense is closely related to story. The author creates suspense in the beginning when he locks the conflict. The reader will be in a constant state of suspense until the conflict is resolved toward the end. This suspense is created primarily through action, and although it is important for the storyline, a deeper form of suspense must be present if the reader is to become fully involved.

In serious fiction, the highest form of suspense involves the "anguish of choice," and the anguish will not come just from worrying over the outcome, but from worrying about the moral implications of the outcome. Through these moral implications, the suspense is directly connected to the Premise, perhaps indelibly etched in Premise. The reader is then brought directly into the story as he worries over the choice himself, whether he would have the courage to make that choice, and how it might eventually affect his life if he did. The suspense builds throughout the novel to the second plot point (3/4 of the way through the novel) at which the protagonist makes the decision and the rest of it plays out to the conclusion.

Although some may think it is a silly little book about a bird, Richard Bach's *Jonathan Livingston Seagull* illustrates the anguish of choice perfectly. The search for perfection in flight leads the little seagull on a spiritual quest that costs him respect within his community and leads him to being cast out of his group. But it also results in a spiritual rebirth. Here, character and Premise are perfectly in tune.

In *Titanic*, as the ship sinks, Rose has to make the ultimate choice of whether to leave aboard the escape boat and remain tied to her fiancée or stay behind with Jack. We feel her anguish as she steps aboard the boat with her mother and the very bondage her mother represents, only at the last moment to jump back aboard the sinking Titanic to be with Jack, making her choice for freedom even at the possible cost of her own life. As she agonizes, we sense the moral implications of her leaving Jack behind. Somehow it just doesn't seem right, and when she jumps back aboard the sinking Titanic, the audience screams with delight. The universe is back in sync.

DIALOGUE

Dialogue, conversation between characters, can't be written the way people speak in real life. The author can't take dictation from real life conversations and paste it on his characters' conversations. Dialogue must be portrayed, sketched, depicted, "characterized." It has to go through the conversion process from the actual into the fictional world, just the same as do all other elements of the novel. Everything is magnified.

But the biggest problem an author has with dialogue is that all of it is coming from the author's own mental processes. All actual conversations occur between two or more people, which means that they come from at least two completely different mental processes. Consider the following dialogue:

> "What did you do today?"
> "I went to the bank."
> "What did you do there?"
> "Deposited three-hundred dollars."
> "How much do we have now?"
> "Four-thousand dollars."

Notice how linear both sides of the conversation are. Each bit of dialogue follows the question–answer, question–answer format. It's simply a process of information gathering. This is a sure sign that one person invented both sides of the conversation. People don't speak that way, particularly people who are in conflict. Consider this revised bit of dialogue:

> "What did you do today?"
> "Why do you want to know?"
> "I'm just curious."
> "I went to the bank."
> "But I went yesterday. How much did you withdraw?"
> "I didn't. I deposited."

Narration

"How much and where did you get it?"

"I put it in my personal account, and it's none of your business."

"Yeah, well you owe me big time, buster, and if you have the money, I want to be paid."

You can see from this example that the two characters have totally separate agendas and are in conflict. Eventually, the same information may come out, but in the meantime, the two characters may be coming close to blows.

Keep in mind that characters speak to express themselves emotionally. Dialogue should capture that emotion, and the author should realize that each character is in a different emotional and intellectual state. A good exercise is to analyze the dialogue in novels you admire. Pay particular attention to the way they sidestep each other's questions or possibly change the topic of the conversation completely.

NARRATIVE COMMENTS

The reader is interested in what happened, not what the author, and rarely what the narrator, thinks about it. The narrator might get away with a narrative comment if his opinion affects the storyline. Describing a beautiful sunset is not a narrative comment, but stating that the sunset is beautiful is. The difference is that the reader is given the opportunity to see the sunset by way of the description and can form his own opinion of it as described, but being told it is beautiful prohibits the reader from forming an opinion. Thus, the narrator should generally get his point across with narrative technique rather than narrative statement.

Narration

THE STORY TOLD TO SOMEONE OTHER THAN THE READER

Sometimes the story is told to another person, possibly as a series of letters, or to no one, as in a diary. Take Alice Walker's *The Color Purple* for instance:

> Dear God,
> I am fourteen years old. I have always been a good girl. Maybe you can give me a sign letting me know what is happening to me.
> Last spring after little Lucious came I heard them fussing. He was pulling on her arm. She say It too soon, Fonso, I ain't well. Finally he leave her alone. A week go by, he pulling on her arm again. She say Now, I ain't gonna. Can't you see I'm already half dead, an all of these children.[29]

This Pulitzer Prize winning novel is written entirely as letters to God. This shows the desperation of the character, but also leaves the reader with a sense of eavesdropping on a confessional. The narrator gains credibility addressing God and baring her soul.

★

The number of different forms of narration is very large, and the author can undoubtedly find a technique that no one has tried. For example, you could construct a story pieced together from emails taken from a murdered person's recovered hard drive. What is absolutely necessary, however, is that the technique match the story. Walker's narrator was in a desperate situation, and her letters to God were an appropriate choice.

To select the best narration, you must know your story before starting to write. Don't start until you know what you are doing.

Narration

EXERCISES

(a) Develop the POV you wish to use in your novel, and provide a description of the POV character(s) and the narrative stance planned for the novel. (b) Select the tense and provide a justification for it. (c) Describe how the narrator and the nature of the story dictate that choice. (d) Provide two double-spaced pages written in the narrative voice.

CHAPTER 5: Irony

Creating the fictional world is difficult. Sometimes, no matter how brilliant your writing, it just doesn't seem to jell. You provide exquisite description, active, intelligent characters, and yet the novel won't come to life. Nothing seems to work, and just when you're about to throw up your hands in despair, it's all so hopeless, along comes one little word to save the day: irony. Irony is your Superman, Wonder Woman and cavalry that will come to the rescue.

The problem is that human reality is much stranger and more complex than you might think, and what you've overlooked is this sticky, existential stuff that goes a long way toward holding it together. The human condition has an ironic edge. And although irony may seem obscure and limited, it's actually a huge, complex subject, and very well may be the single most important subject for the novelsmith who has mastered the elements of plot, character, and narration.

All right then. What is irony?

Irony is generally thought of as simply saying the opposite of what is meant. When someone says, "And the wonderful weather continues," following a week of fog and rain, we know that the person is speaking ironically. Irony might also be said to be the mismatch between appearance and reality, between what is expected and the actual occurrence. In *The Lord of the Rings*, when Frodo, a meek little hobbit, offers the ultimate ring of power to Gandalf, an immortal wizard and one of the most powerful beings in Middle Earth, for safekeeping, Frodo doesn't get the "thank you" he expects, but instead, shock and horror from Gandalf. Understanding this one short episode exposes the naiveté of the Hobbits, the inherent goodness of Gandalf and the nature of absolute power, who can be allowed to possess it and who can't. The use of irony here helps to expose the full meaning behind the lengthy story and provides insight into the characters. But don't get too fixated on irony as an opposite. The most important aspect is the meaningful disconnect.

Even in the time of Plato and Socrates, irony was associated with saying something that was not meant literally. The word "irony" comes from the ancient Greek εἰρωνεια (eironeia), which means "assumed [feigned] ignorance."[30] Perhaps the first story in western literature containing irony comes from Hesiod, who flourished around 750 BC. As described in his *Works and Days*, when Zeus learned that Prometheus had stolen fire and given it to mankind, Zeus roared with laughter.[31] He laughed, not because mankind was going to do something funny with fire, but because he saw the irony of the situation. Prometheus had given mankind fire to keep us from dwindling into nonexistence, but Zeus knew the trail of misery it would cause. Thus, Prometheus' act was ironic. This has become a metaphor for all scientific achievement, because scientific "advances" frequently cause new problems, and sometimes these problems become larger than those the advances solved. Also note that this anecdote tells us something about character. Zeus understood the implications of Prometheus' act while Prometheus didn't. More about this below.

Irony

This example from Hesiod also illustrates one of the more curious and helpful aspects of irony. Irony is frequently considered to be witty or funny. Zeus saw the irony in Prometheus' act, and it caused him to laugh even though what was about to happen wasn't funny. Indeed, practically all humor comes from the many faces of irony. This may seem to be an overstatement, but once you see all of its ramifications, you may also come to understand this to be true.

This particular example also illustrates something else about irony, and to understand it, we must delve a little deeper into Greek mythology. Prometheus was a Titan, one of the generations of gods that came before Zeus. The word "titan" was derived from the Greek "τιταινειν," which means to overreach, and was used as an insult.[32] The Titan intellect was one of creativity and ingenuity, but the Titans' lack of wisdom prevented them from seeing the ramifications of their actions. Titans had no feel for irony. The generation of gods under Zeus, the Olympians, were known for their wisdom. They had not only the intellect to solve problems, but also the wisdom to foresee the implications. Zeus could see the outcome of Prometheus giving mankind fire, but Prometheus couldn't; therefore, Zeus had an ironic stance, which came about because of his wisdom.

In this way, Irony can be viewed as a perspective. Colebrook describes the ironic perspective:

> Irony exists 'above' existence, giving the world form. Irony is the adoption of a point of view 'above' a context, allowing us to view the context from 'on high'.[33]

We can see this even in the simplest form of verbal irony. The fact that someone says the weather is good, and yet we understand that he means it is bad, indicates that we understand the statement in a broader context. Human beings don't much appreciate rain and snow in their everyday lives. The tone of the speaker may also confirm the opposite as the reality. This is the context that allows us to interpret the statement ironically. If a farmer in the middle of a drought made the statement about a rainstorm, however, we'd probably interpret it as a simple statement of fact.

Irony, then, alludes to a truth that transcends language[34] and demands more of the reader, that he have a certain wisdom enabling him to recognize a subtext that carries the meaning rather than the literal words. This intellectual demand pulls the reader more deeply into the story, and the story seems more connected. Characters who make ironic statements about each other, e.g., "That nun gives of herself like a hooker," are more connected to the world around them. Whether this speaker has used an ironic but tasteless metaphor or is stating a literal fact is something the reader will determine by investigating the character speaking, the character spoken about, and the context.

Considerable trouble in translating and interpreting ancient texts has resulted from cases in which the social context of a statement is uncertain or not known at all. But Socrates' use of irony has been discussed since Aristotle, so that the context of his statements within Plato's dialogues was well-established in antiquity, and this fact enables us to get at his true meaning. Indeed, one of the reasons irony captured the interest of the academic community is that Socrates used irony in his dialogues as a method of uncovering truth on the great issues of his time.

At this point you might be thinking that this irony stuff is a rather elitist phenomenon and that your readership might not be up to the task of interpreting it. This is hardly the case. Just remember Aesop's famous fable of the tortoise and the hare, the slow tortoise that wins the race against the lightning-quick hare. And as an example from real life for animal lovers, anyone who has ever owned a dog knows how they like to play tug-rope. They pull viciously on one end of the rope while you pull on the other, and the dog will growl as though he wants to bite your head off. But let go and walk off, and he'll whine and bring the rope to you, begging to do it again. His growl didn't mean that he was angry, but indeed, he somehow meant the opposite. Lions, tigers, and bears, however, are somewhat slow on the uptake when it comes to irony, so don't try tug-rope with them.

When all is said and done, irony comes to everyone intuitively, and it's just the intellectualizing of it that gets rather complicated. Recognizing irony is one thing, but using it as an active force within a novel is quite another. For an author frowning over a pedestrian piece of narration, introducing a little irony just might be the salt that makes the French fries worth eating. The trick is not to force irony into the story, but to find the irony within the situations being portrayed and bring it to the surface.

In the paragraphs to follow, I will discuss authorial uses of irony that effect dialogue, character, plot, Premise, and one more use that originates when the narrator takes the reader into his confidence, dramatic irony. I'll even go one step further and investigate how irony can allude to a meaning that lies beyond the story itself. If the author can accomplish this last step, the novel can shimmer with significance. With this accomplished, the reader won't be able to let go of the novel even if he's read it a couple of times.

VERBAL IRONY

Irony

This is simply dialogue, characters saying the opposite of what they mean, as in the earlier weather example. But verbal irony isn't always an opposite. Sometimes, for example, it comes as an exaggeration. Remember, irony is a disconnect. When a narrator says, "None of the other instructors at the university seemed to notice something that the professor's students detected about him immediately—the man didn't have a brain," we know the narrator is speaking ironically. Obviously, a professor at a center of learning has a brain, but we also know that he must have some rather startling deficiencies. The reader's interest is immediately peaked because he's going to be asked to solve the mystery surrounding this man's intellect. Inherent in this one bit of narration are both irony of reversal and exaggeration. The reversal comes because generally professors are really smart and this man is probably an exception. The exaggeration comes because we know that, if the man can walk and talk, he must have a brain. The context can take us in another direction, though, if the professor is an android in a science fiction novel. So context, this higher plane of knowing, is crucial to making sense of the narrative.

THE IRONIC CHARACTER

For character development, the author might envision an ironic character, whose pattern of dealing with people might be the following:

As a figure or extended mode of thought irony allows the speaker to remain 'above' what he says, allowing those members of his audience who share his urbanity to perceive the true sense of what is really meant.[35]

Irony

Thus, the character might be rather snobbish and not prone to speaking at a level where his ideas can be easily understood, much the way Socrates dealt with those whose opinions he argued against without divulging his own. This is characterization of the intellect, the way the character thinks and deals with ideas and other people. This is only one way to exploit irony in characterization. A creative novelsmith could find all sorts of ways to develop character personality using this new tool.

Characters may also have "external" ironic behavior patterns. Ironic behavior may be quickly identified in the local and national headlines, and it is not always humorous. One quick example is the Catholic priest who molests children. The disconnect between his professional life and personal conduct manifests in tragedy for his victims. Still, the irony of these characters' lives makes for a strange, curious quality that draws the reader into the story, much like people slowing down and gawking at a roadside accident.

Socrates saw our world, the "real" world, as only a metaphor of divine existence. Divine existence was viewed as a mystery that could never be fully understood by human beings. Socrates used irony to expose our understanding as being always incomplete and to allude to the complete divine truth that could only be experienced through a sort of intellectual peripheral vision. Socrates was always trying to pull back the curtain to enable us to see the wizard at work, to use a metaphor from *The Wizard of Oz*. Thus the ironic perspective itself, according to some, is rather divine and exists "above" human existence.

Characters who don't have irony as a part of their makeup tend to be dogmatic, literal and not very easy to get along with. The man who is without irony is not looking for answers. He already knows the answers. However, he is most susceptible to irony of fate. The ironic man is looking for answers. He is not so attached to his opinions, not even this world actually, and has a sort of wisdom that transcends his own nature. Indeed, as mentioned before wisdom itself may require irony.[36]

PLOT IRONY/COSMIC IRONY

To illustrate cosmic irony, consider its occurrence in what is possibly the most famous play in the history of literature, Sophocles' *Oedipus Tyrannus*. The play, written in 429 BC, concerns the fate of the king of Thebes, a city-state to the north of Athens, during the mythological Mycenaean era, ~1250 BC. When the play opens, Oedipus is king and his kingdom is faced with a plague that is decimating the entire area. He consults the Delphic Oracle to find the reason for the plague, and learns that Thebes is harboring the murderer of the previous king, Laius. Harboring the murderer has polluted the city, and the killer must be found and brought to justice to end the plague. Oedipus vows to find the murderer and sets off to bring him to justice.

Through the course of the play, we learn that years before, Oedipus had been a prince at Corinth, son of the king, but left Corinth as a result of an oracle received at Delphi saying that he would kill his father and marry his mother. He then refused to return to Corinth and instead went to Thebes where, as the result of a series of bizarre events, he was made king and given the hand of the queen, Jocasta, in marriage. The plague followed some twenty years later. Also, during his attempt to learn the identity of the murderer, Jocasta tells him that Laius, her previous husband, was killed at a crossroads shortly before Oedipus himself had come to Thebes. Oedipus then tells her that he had killed a man at that

Irony

same crossroads while on his way to Thebes. But Jocasta says that Laius was killed by a band of robbers, so that it couldn't have been the same man.

Coincidentally, a messenger then arrives from Corinth to tell Oedipus that his father has passed away. Oedipus expresses relief because he'd escaped the oracle that had said he was to kill his father and marry his mother. But the messenger tells Oedipus that there was never any danger of that because he'd been adopted. The rumors Oedipus had heard years before were true. Oedipus soon learned that Laius and Jocasta had once had a child, which the Delphic oracle had said would kill Laius, so they had the child exposed on a mountainside and left to die. But a shepherd had saved the child, and taken him to Corinth, where the king had adopted him as his own. Oedipus was that child, and sure enough he'd killed his father, his biological father, and married his biological mother.

The irony in the plot of this story is that Oedipus, by trying to avoid the fate predicted by the oracle, fulfilled it. This is known as "cosmic irony" or "irony of fate," which is sort of a "conspiracy of the elements" that produce a predestined result. It is also "irony of reversal," because the outcome is the opposite of what Oedipus intended by his actions.

Irony in this particular myth has several reflections. From Laius' standpoint, he got rid of the son who would grow up to kill him, only to set up a situation that would lead to his death. Also, Oedipus blinded himself after realizing what he'd done. Oedipus, when blind, could finally see who he really was for the first time, and while he had been able see, he had been blind to his own identity.

This irony concerning blindness and internal vision is a famil-

Irony

iar theme in Greek myth. Teiresias, the blind seer at Thebes, could see the future and had warned Oedipus of what was about to happen. Teiresias had been blinded years before for seeing the goddess Athena naked, but she gave him "internal" sight as recompense. Teiresias is an ironic character. Irony is a sort of twist in logic and, as in Oedipus' case, it can also be an underlying plot structure.

DRAMATIC IRONY

Dramatic irony is a rather curious narrative technique involving the relationship between the narrator and the reader. Dramatic irony occurs when the narrator takes the reader into his confidence and tells him something that the characters do not know. Colebrook defines it this way:

> If the audience sees or knows more than a character, or if a character's speech is undermined by subsequent action, then we can say that there is a dramatic irony, an irony that plays on a disjunction between character and audience point of view.[37]

As an example, consider the generic scene from a horror story wherein the naive heroine enters a dark room, and the reader cringes with terror because he knows that a murderer is hiding behind the door. This increases the tension for the reader, and it can become so intense that he may have to put the book down for a minute and say to himself, "This is only a novel. This is only a novel."

CONCLUSION

To capture the full human experience and sense the divine element that is so elusive, a novel needs some degree of ironic

Irony

stance. Whether irony will be visible to the reader depends on narrative technique and how close the narrator is to the action. As we live life, rarely do we see the irony of our own existence; therefore, in a first-person narration, cosmic irony may be more deeply buried than in third person. With distance from the action, we gain the perspective necessary to view it ironically.

The more you come to terms with irony, the better chance you have of getting an accurate portrayal of life itself. Just as the five senses help construct physical reality, irony is an overarching sense of understanding, a deeper understanding. This comes from an intellectual evaluation of the story that makes it more interesting and brings it closer to actual human experience.

Again, irony is a difficult, complex subject but important enough to learn as much about as possible. A novel, by its very nature, strives to reveal an ultimate truth, something that exists on a plane above normal existence. Socrates thought it alluded to something in the divine world. This is the ironic stance, and, therefore, all novels are ironic. To further explore this subject, see the highly recommended *Irony* by Claire Colebrook.

EXERCISES
(a) Define your overall strategy for using irony, whether it is to play a primary or secondary role in your novel. (b) Identify ironic aspects of your storyline. (c) Write a paragraph on how you think a reader's perception of your novel might be different from your own.

CHAPTER 6: The Fictional World

THE GRAND ILLUSION

When a reader picks up a novel, he "signs" a contract with the author. The author has already fulfilled his part of the contract: to present the story as truth. The reader's part then is to suspend disbelief. So the author and the reader are accomplices in deceit. This is what I call "The Grand Illusion." The novelsmith creates an entirely fictional world through suggestion, and the reader agrees not only to believe it, but to recreate it, or the illusion of it, in his own mind. This begs the question: How do we, as novelsmiths, create our fictional world? We can find the answer by investigating how we as human beings "create" the real physical world. Once we understand how human beings relate to the real world, we can then adapt that relationship to fiction.

It may come as a shock to some that we actually do not have direct contact with the physical world. The real world comes to us through the five senses: touch, taste, sight, sound, and smell. The information from the five senses is sent to the brain where it "creates" a *perception* of the "real" world. Note that I say a *perception* of the world rather than the actual world. Human beings are always divorced from reality and subject to the limitations of the senses. This then is our clue to creating the fictional world. We must somehow "stimulate" the reader's five senses to get him to experience the fictional physical world.

READER SENSORY DEPRIVATION

This is where we leave behind not only the real world but also cinema. As human beings, we experience the real world through the five senses: sight, sound, smell, touch, and taste. Light enters our eyes, stimulates the optic nerve, and is interpreted by our brain to produce an image. The other four senses act similarly. So actually, we do not experience the real world but create it in our minds from the stimulation of our senses. Movies exploit two of these: sight and sound. Movies are easy. They come at you. But the reader has no active senses in the fictional world, and the author must stimulate the reader's senses by evoking them to create that world. The reader has an equally difficult job. He has to "find" the world of the novel within his imagination by allowing the words to evoke his senses.

Consequently, the technique for writing a novel is radically different from that of writing a screenplay. A screenplay is a road-map for stimulating the viewer's sight and sound senses. To stimulate the other three senses (feel, touch and taste), the screenwriter must use visual images and sound. In the *Alien* movie series, starring Sigourney Weaver, the viewer gets a vivid "feel" for the monster because it secretes sticky fluids and when wounded leaks acid, but we never get a sense of smell because the characters never react to an aroma.

Reading is like no other human activity. As just stated, we create the real world through input to our senses. But in the fictional world, the reader experiences *total sensory deprivation*. Though the reader uses sight to read the novel, he cannot literally see the fictional world as he does in a movie. To assist the reader in creating the illusion of reality, the narrator must evoke the senses. The more senses you bring to bear on the story, the more the fictional world seems real and the greater the impact. You can tell a reader that your character is a little girl and show her pigtails and the sprinkle of freckles across the bridge of her nose, but until you smell the peanut butter on her breath and feel the heat of her little hands, she won't be fully alive.

For the purposes of this discussion, let's split the senses into two categories: those we experience as "out there" in the external world, and those we experience as internal, within our own bodies. The "external" senses are sight and sound. These two are perceived, seem to "happen," outside ourselves. Though an image appears to be outside the eye, it actually is constructed from light entering the eye. Additionally, we never see an object; we see light reflected from it. Similarly with sound, we don't hear a drum beat; we construct the sound from vibratory data received from the fluctuation of air pressure on the eardrum. (Of course, this view of sight and sound as "external" has its limits because looking at the sun will cause physical pain in the eye if not done through a light-limiting device, and a really loud sound can hurt the ears.) To deepen the emotional impact, we turn to the other three senses, which I'll refer to as being "internal."

The "internal" senses are taste, smell and touch. These senses are personal in that they are experienced more directly. You have to actually ingest a little of a substance to either taste or smell it. This can require a little risk-taking and trust because some substances, by virtue of even a small dose, can cause illness or even death. Smell occurs inside the nose. To feel something, to touch it, it must come into contact with your skin or physically move part of your body. You can feel the heat when a person touches your arm or the take-off acceleration of an airplane by the pressure on your entire body. Taste only occurs in the mouth and thus is the most personal of all the senses. These three senses, taken together, can have a greater emotional impact on the reader than can sight and sound.

The mind is so susceptible to images and sounds, so practiced at focusing on them, that the writer hardly has to evoke them at all. We humans have a propensity to visualize, which evokes the "internal" senses and seems to cause the mind to hallucinate. Smell, taste and touch, however, are the most neglected by writers. These "forgotten" senses work more on the subconscious. The taste of a woman's lipstick may call up sexual images: lips, breasts, thighs; the smell of a rotting carcass conjures images of maggots, leathery skin and bones, bringing home the finality of death.

Perhaps the most important effect of evoking these more subtle senses is the narrative closeness it creates with character. Touch is particularly effective in bringing the reader right inside a character. This feeling property is also connected with the emotions, the feelings of a character, so much so that the word "feeling" is used for both the physical sensation and the emotional state. A character can feel cold or fear, and both are called feelings, but each has radically different internal manifestations. Since these three are so personal and relate so strongly to the internal state of the character, they can have a more powerful emotional effect on the reader, at times causing him to hallucinate.

Sound should also not be forgotten as a hallucinatory agent. In the right context, the tinkle of breaking glass means trouble: domestic violence, robbery, or bloody gashes. But remember that it may not dig as deeply into your character and won't into your reader either.

The Fictional World

EVOKING THE SENSES

The chief attributes of all the senses are quality, intensity, and duration. Identifying more than just the quality of the sense (a sweet taste, a soft sound) gives it the dimension of being active, that it has affected the character. A woman who has just burned her finger on the stove knows the intensity and duration of that feeling. She'll suck her finger to remove heat, and it'll burn for hours, hurt for days, and may even leave a scar.

As another example, consider the blacksmith who has just smashed his thumb with a hammer so hard that he has knocked the nail loose. The throbbing pain (quality) of the thumb and shooting pain up the arm (quality) is almost unbearable (intensity), but also the pain seems to go on indefinitely (duration). He reaches immediately for the painkiller, while visualizing a sleepless night and the days and weeks to come (duration) working with an injured thumb. Notice nothing has been stated about the dull thump of the hammer on the thumb (sound) or the dangling nail and dripping blood (sight), but you as the reader probably saw it all and heard the hammer hit the thumb.

The tactile sense is easy to describe (smooth, rough, soft, slimy), but how do you describe a smell or taste? Generally, you'll have to rely on reader memory. You only have to mention strawberries to get the taste. To get the smell of coffee you can rely on the way steam wafts up from the cup, or you can tell your reader "the woman has coffee breath." In that way, the "action" of a smell can be essential for the reader to experience it. Also, look for cross-coupling of the senses. You can smell a fish better if you're reminded of that slimy slickness.

The senses don't just exist, and just describing a smell, taste or touch isn't enough. The senses are active. A smell can emanate from a room, or a man's body odor seep through his clothes and waft about him as he walks from person to person. In fiction, the senses must have an impact on the character and produce a reaction. It's hard to smell a rose without smiling, unless allergies cause you to sneeze. A whiff of decaying carcass can produce a reaction described as "turning up the nose." Keep your characters reacting to their sensory experience, but also realize that the senses can be used to develop character. Being nearsighted or farsighted is rather common, but important. A blind man's heightened sense of smell when it's crucial to survival can have dramatic implications.

As an example of the power of the senses, consider the movie, *Silence of the Lambs*. The first time Clarice goes to see Hannibal Lecter in prison, he tells her that he can tell her menstrual cycle by her smell. This is a real invasion of privacy, and lets us know how vulnerable she is to the man behind bars. Also, at the end of the movie, Clarice enters the home of the serial killer, where it is totally dark. She puts on infrared goggles that enable her to partially see in the dark. This limitation on her vision causes a palpable anxiety in the viewer. She also breathes through a mask that makes her breathing labored and noisy, and the combination of vision impairment and a sense of partial suffocation increases the anxiety in the viewer to a point where it's practically unbearable.

Evoking the senses is an extensive subject, and noticing the techniques of master storytellers is crucial to developing your own skill. Here's a passage from Hemingway:

> They were walking through the heather of the mountain meadow and Robert Jordan felt the brushing of the heather against his legs, felt the weight of his pistol in its holster against

his thigh, felt the sun on his head, felt the breeze from the snow of the mountain peaks cool on his back and, in his hand, he felt the girl's hand firm and strong, the fingers locked in his. From it, from the palm of her hand against the palm of his, from their fingers locked together, and from her wrist across his wrist something came from her hand, her fingers and her wrist to his that was as fresh as the first light air that moving toward you over the sea barely wrinkles the glass surface of a calm, as light as a feather moved across one's lip, or a leaf falling when there is no breeze; so light that it could be felt with the touch of their fingers alone, but that was so strengthened, so intensified, and made so urgent, so aching and so strong by the hard pressure of their fingers and the close pressed palm and wrist, that it was as though a current moved up his arm and filled his whole body with an aching hollowness of wanting.[38]

This is an astounding piece of writing, all of it evoking a single sense, touch, and it produces an emotional reaction in the last sentence: "an aching hollowness of wanting." Hemingway connects the reader not only with the outside world, but also with the internal, emotional landscape of his character. He marries touch with emotion, which makes the work instantly accessible because we all have contact with the outside world through touch.

While editing your work during the rewrite stage, find ways to integrate the senses into the narrative. Concentrate on those critical to the point-of-view character. One last passage from Hemingway:

Pablo had gone in out of sight in the cave. Robert Jordan

hoped he had gone for food. He sat on the ground by the gypsy and the afternoon sunlight came down through the tree tops and was warm on his outstretched legs. He could smell food now in the cave, the smell of oil and of onions and of meat frying and his stomach moved with hunger inside of him.[39]

Notice how Hemingway's character responds to other characters and his environment. We not only get the character's connection to the outside world, but also with his own stomach.

The key to creating this type of fiction is to realize that your reader suffers from total sensory deprivation. The author responding to this reader disadvantage will put him on the right path to creating powerful fiction. Take for example this excerpt from Ray Bradbury's *The Martian Chronicles*:

It was a long road going into darkness and hills and he held to the wheel, now and again reaching into his lunch bucket and taking out a piece of candy. He had been driving steadily for an hour, with no other car on the road, no light, just the road going under, the hum, the roar, and Mars out there, so quiet. Mars was always quiet, but quieter tonight than any other. The deserts and empty seas swung by him, and the mountains against the stars.

There was a smell of Time in the air tonight. He smiled and turned the fancy in his mind. There was a thought. What did Time smell like? Like dust and clocks and people. And if you wondered what Time sounded like it sounded like water running in a dark cave and voices crying and dirt dropping down upon hollow box lids, and rain. And, going further, what did Time *look* like? Time looked like snow dropping silently into a black room or it looked like a silent film in an ancient theater, one hundred billion faces falling like those New Year balloons, down and down into nothing. That was how Time smelled and looked and sounded. And tonight—Tomas shoved a hand into the wind outside the truck—tonight you could almost *touch* Time.[40]

Bradbury mingles ideas with sensory detail until the reader can feel time. He sees the world, not as a physicist would lay out the facts about time, but as a poet sees it. This is the organic unity of craft and art that the novelsmith brings to his work through narration, always stretching fictional reality until it almost matches the strangeness of the human experience. This is the essence of good narration, and the author must make use of both his narrative sense and his ability to create reality through the use of the senses.

Another powerful sense that can really bring fiction to life is the sixth sense, which manifests as a sense of anticipation, as in a sense of foreboding before a catastrophe. This is different than foreshadowing and is directly coupled with a character's ability to assess a situation and intuit a result, to anticipate the future.

★

So this is the fictional world wherein the novel resides. But there is another world, one more deeply embedded within the novel, that provides meaning. That is the intellectual world, and now is the time to visit it.

EXERCISES:

(a) Lists the settings in your storyline where you believe it will be most important for reader to be sensually connected to your fictional world. (b) Within each of these settings, identify the primary sense you will need to evoke. (c) Identify the times when a character's sixth sense might be important.

CHAPTER 7: The Intellectual World

Meaning is so much a part of everyday life that it has become like the air we breathe: ever-present but never really part of our awareness. Yet, meaning is what drives our lives, and without it, life is hardly bearable. The same is true of a novel. It must be instilled with meaning but that meaning will require conscious scrutiny to discern it. If the novel contains little to provide meaning, it is a jumble of uninteresting events.

Some novels ooze meaning. Dostoevsky's novels are jammed with ideas, and his characters write papers, letters, notes, and argue the great controversies of their time, ranging from the intellectually sublime to the trivialities of human existence. In *The Brothers Karamazov,* one of the brothers, Alyosha, is studying for the priesthood; Dmitri is sensual, impulsive and poetic; Ivan, the atheist intellectual; and Smerdyakov, the illegitimate epileptic. The father is a wicked and sentimental old profligate. The interactions of these characters, clashes really, produce an amazingly rich philosophical novel. But even with Dostoevsky, the reader still struggles to identify the author's ultimate purpose, the overriding meaning behind the novel. A novel must, indeed, have a central meaning, although, as Dostoevsky shows us, the novelsmith should make his reader look for it.

To convey the nature of meaning within storytelling, let's turn to Giorgio de Santillana. In his prologue to *The Origins of Scientific Thought*, he gives the following example:

> There is an Indian tale to explain the difference between organic and inorganic. The stone and the pumpkin had a quarrel about their respective merits. The stone at last jumped on the pumpkin and smashed it, hoping to prove its point. But right then the offshoots of the pumpkin burst forth in blossom. The price of life is death and vice versa.[41]

In this short excerpt, de Santillana not only tells a story, but also gives his interpretation of the purpose of the story upfront, and then further interprets it after telling it. This, in a nutshell, is the experience of reading a novel. De Santillana carries his discussion one step further, however, by addressing the very nature of this type of storytelling:

> "If we face it [life itself] as a problem, it leads nowhere. As a myth, it carries its own acceptance.
>
> This kind of explaining is surely not science; it implies no theory or definition; but it is a kind of knowledge: mythical knowledge, which means explaining something by telling a tale about it which should show it in the light of an essential truth. The story of Genesis is such a myth."[42]

This is what the author is after: to construct a tale that contains within it an essential truth. The novel is a long narrative form that performs the same service as de Santillana's simple story. At the core of the novel is this bit of "mythical knowledge" that the author exposes as "an essential truth." This, once again, draws us back to Premise.

The reader experiences meaning within the pages of a novel, both because of the author's effort, and because of the way he, the reader, interprets the work. The author injects the work with meaning through the use of ideas, storyline structure, and the juxtaposition of ordered events (plotting). And second, the reader contemplates the work, interpreting the information to extract meaning. Thus, the total process is inexact by its very nature, thank goodness, and perhaps allows the reader to interpret the work somewhat differently than the author intended. Consequently, some readers will love it, others hate it, and yet others will be indifferent about it.

In a nutshell, this then is the intellectual world of the novel. It is a world of ideas, and during this short chapter we will explore the intellectual world, and how to create and control it as much as possible. A novel is a storehouse of focused ideas, interrelated by the context of the novel. The author must limit the cast of ideas because extraneous ideas lack pertinence and generate confusion in the reader. Ideas are focused, not just to provide clarity, but also meaning, and the intellectual world of the novel is a "world of meaning." The novelsmith hones his work to address only those ideas that pertain to the central subject and thus only those of the central conflict.

MEANING

Everyday events, with their smooth-flowing, continuous action as well as their fits and starts, contain no meaning. It isn't until the mind interprets the events that meaning is introduced. Meaning exists in that ironic stance that exists in the intellectual mist above the story. Meaning is always present in a story, though, because story comes from the interpretation of life. Even if you don't intend your story to mean anything, something will still be there in your unconscious piecing-together of the story and in the reader's mind as he interprets it. Meaning is inherent in the nature of storytelling, in the juxtaposition of events and in the relationships between characters. The initial way you consciously interject meaning into your story is through, of course, Premise.

To convey meaning, the novel must speak on the level of revelation. What constitutes the state of containing meaning is elusive, but a novel starts to lose meaning if, through loosely connected scenes, it becomes episodic as opposed to being driven by cause-and-effect. Working from a Premise tends to keep the novel from becoming episodic, and instills it with meaning since conflict is always center stage and results in cause-and-effect scenarios. Consider this discussion:

> "Why did you hit him?"
> "Because he offended me."
> "How did he offend you?"
> "He spit on my shoe."
> "Why did he spit on your shoe?"
> "Because I slept with his wife."
> "Why did you sleep with a married woman?"
> "Marriage doesn't mean a lot to me."

In this snippet of conversation, we can see cause-and-effect and how the conflict described starts to reveal meaning. The conflict arises because of the differing perceptions of marriage, and it results in a sequence of events that follow a cause-and-effect scenario. The meaning of the story will be revealed by the outcome of the conflict and will make a statement about marriage. As the conflict unfolds, the reader would expect to see the many sides of marriage and perhaps how other marriages relate to the "outside" world. Meaning will come about through the conflict and resolution inherent in the author's Premise concerning marriage.

Carl Jung believed that, with the birth of an individual, "a question enters the world, to which he must provide some kind of answer." Of his own life, Jung said:

> The meaning of my existence is that life has addressed a question to me. Or, conversely, I myself am a question which is addressed to the world...[43]

If we return to the analogy of the novel as a life, with a birth and a death, we can now see that it also comes into the world as a question. In the same way, meaning comes into the story through Premise. Though steeped in conflict, its essence is a question. The Premise is an answer to the universal question.

The theme of a novel is frequently defined as "what it's about," but as we saw earlier, this doesn't really say much. Webster's defines theme as "the subject" of a literary work, but "subject" is also too ambiguous to be helpful. Theme isn't about plot, but is, in fact, the defining feature of the intellectual world of the novel. Searching for theme is much like searching for Premise. The two are closely related, and we have frequently referred to them as synonymous in this book. You will, at some point, determine your own definition, but I will define theme here as, "The philosophical question presented by the central conflict."

Now that you're really confused, and at the risk of leaving you in a terminal state of bewilderment, we're going to leave the discussion there. The closer you look at some subjects, the more blurred they become. While you're putting your novel together, just be aware that if you don't know what it's about, in the intellectual sense, neither will your reader.

EXERCISES
(a) Identify the major idea that is exposed by your Premise. (b) List the secondary ideas you will explore in your novel. (c) Write a paragraph on what your novel means.

CHAPTER 8: Chapters

A novel is a structure of structures.[44] At the beginning of this book, we started with the broadest overall structure, the Premise, progressed through the more detailed Novel Diagram with its plot points and reversal, and now we break down the diagram into its component parts: chapters. Before directors start to make a movie, they storyboard, i.e., lay out all the important scenes in hand-drawn pictures. The comparable step for the novelsmith is to provide a one paragraph summary for each chapter. This gives the author an opportunity to establish pace and ensure a logical scene sequence.

To return to the analogy of a novel as a house, a house has walls that function structurally but also divide the home into functional rooms where the people live: bedrooms, kitchen, living room, etc. Just as houses have rooms, novels have chapters within which characters act out their lives. And just as each room in a house has a specific purpose, each chapter has its own agenda. Certain things must happen in the first chapter: specifically it must lock the central conflict. A later chapter will dramatize the First Plot Point, etc.

In creating chapter summaries, the author has the first opportunity to use his selected narrative voice and tense. The summaries can be written without doing this, but if you do, they'll help ensure that you don't deviate from the POV. All character introductions, plot and subplot events must be put in sequence. Here, the novelsmith must orchestrate the story elements, a role that will become more complex as work on the novel proceeds.

READER IMPACT

Chapters are also about reader breathing space. The reader experiences a sort of claustrophobia if the narrative is one long, uninterrupted stream of discourse. A break from time to time prevents a tiring, perhaps even confusing, reading experience. Reading a novel might be compared to eating an elephant. The end of a chapter gives the reader time to swallow. Similarly, the reader must be given the narrative in bite-sized chunks, so that he can ingest what has just happened and assimilate the profound event that has just occurred. You don't eat an elephant in one sitting. Even though the reader may dig into the next chapter without a break, he has been allowed an emotional break. Chapter length can vary considerably but will generally average ten to fifteen pages. The size of the chapter should fit the subject matter. Don't think the short attention span of the modern American reader resulted in the short chapter. Herman Melville, in *Moby Dick*, which was first published in 1851, wrote a lot of three-page chapters.

CHAPTER PURPOSE

Chapters are about more than enabling a few deep breaths. A long story has its ebbs and flows, its milestones. The elements within a chapter have a tighter relationship than they do with the rest of the novel, and are put together so they constitute a rounded whole. Chapters can also mark different scenes, times and places within the narrative, or possibly a change of subject matter. Each chapter must complete a significant event in the storyline and also reveal more about the central conflict and characters.

CHAPTER SEQUENCE

Logic and cause-and-effect determine chapter sequence. Sometimes the author will skip around in a story, but as a rule stories should have a linear storyline, with events proceeding in what would simulate real life. Not all chapters are created equal or in the same image. Some are used for setting up the story, others for developing conflict and character. Some will carry greater emotional impact and others have a more intellectual bent. The place to start when determining which chapters are absolutely indispensable is the Novel Diagram presented in Chapter 2. Each milestone in the diagram will have at least one chapter devoted to it. Also, the milestones from the character arc diagrams may dictate more chapters. Use storyline progression to determine if you need less or more, combining some, dividing others. Figure 10 shows a possible compilation of chapters for a hypothetical novel.

These days, publishers don't much appreciate novels exceeding 300 pages due to editing time and printing costs. Agents are also reluctant to represent novels, particularly from unpublished authors, greater than this length. A chapter should not exceed approximately fifteen pages; therefore, according to these ground rules, a novel will have approximately twenty chapters. Adhering to these arbitrary restrictions may be difficult for the author to accept. For one's first novel, you would be well advised to conform.

Don't take these restrictions as absolute. Make sure what you decide about chapters fits your material and your perception of your novel. Remember that all suggestions here are intended to remove some of the mystery of novel construction and are not intended to be strictly followed.

Chapters

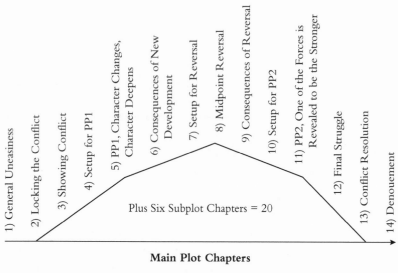

Figure 10

CHAPTER INTERNAL STRUCTURE

First of all, a chapter is not a short story, regardless of how many excerpts you've seen published in short story journals. A chapter is generally so connected and completed by the rest of the novel, that rarely can it stand alone. Because each chapter is uniquely placed and fulfills a specific part of the overall storyline, each will have its own structural requirements. Yet, they do have a beginning, a middle, and an end.

As shown in Figure 11 below, each individual chapter will have a central point that must relate to the overall progression of the storyline. The scene that includes the central point in the chapter should probably be dramatized. The rest may be presented in narrative summary. Each chapter also has thematic (Premise) requirements placed on it, and this gives it a philosophical quality. The end of the first chapter contains the fire that continues to burn in the next chapter.

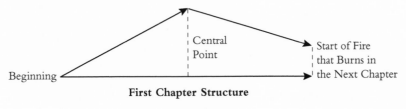

First Chapter Structure

Figure 11

The vertical axis in this diagram is intended to show dramatic tension. Note that it builds to a maximum and then tails off but does not go to zero. Chapters are also like a relay race, as shown in Figure 12. A chapter takes the storyline, advances it a little and passes it off to the next chapter. The storyline is the baton.

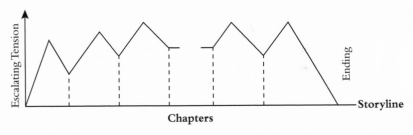

Chapters

Figure 12

Each chapter accepts a certain amount of tension from the previous chapter but carries with it its own tension-building devices. A chapter shouldn't let the tension drop to zero, not even at the end where the basic point of the chapter is concluded. Chapters themselves do have many of the characteristics of a complete story, but the completeness comes more from having satisfied Premise needs at that point rather than storyline progression.

FIRST CHAPTER

The first chapter may well be devoted to locking the central conflict. For a complex story, the author may need one chapter to lock the "background" conflict and another to set up the conflict between characters. In *Titanic*, the background conflict ("Even God couldn't sink the Titanic.") is set up separately from Rose's conflict with her mother and fiancé over getting married. In *The Grapes of Wrath*, Steinbeck uses a four-page first chapter to describe how the weather ushered in the dust bowl of the 1930's, establishing a sort of cosmic conflict between man and God. He introduced his characters in chapter two.

Many times, however, the first chapter is used to present the narrator and characters to the reader. In Waller's *The Bridges of Madison County*, he uses an elaborate scheme in which, as the author, he supposedly receives a woman's journal from her grown children. The author then claims he has pieced together the story from his own research and her journal describing her adultery. Of course, the work is a complete fabrication.

Sometimes, the author will accomplish all the setup in the first chapter. In Fitzgerald's *The Great Gatsby*, he uses the first few pages to let the first-person narrator (Nick) introduce himself and the "hero" of the story (Gatsby). Before the chapter is through, the central conflict is established and all the characters brought into the story. Fitzgerald didn't have any time to waste. *Gatsby* (his masterpiece) was hardly more than 120 pages.

Chapters

LAST CHAPTER

A novel always forms something of a circle. It starts by locking the central conflict, then puts the finishing touches on that same conflict by resolving it at the end. Thus, the ending is intimately tied to the beginning. The author should ensure that all the expectations created in the beginning have been fulfilled. Once the main conflict has been resolved, the author should end the novel as quickly as possible, although American readers do tend to want all the ramifications spelled out. If the author ever has a place to attempt eloquence, this is it. He has the entire weight of the novel behind him.

A word of caution: avoid moralizing. In particular, do not reveal your Premise. Stick to the story, the mood cast by the aftermath of the resolution, and avoid summing it all up. The most skillful novelsmith will leave the moral implications of the story ambiguous. The action will have a definite resolution, the protagonist will either win or lose, but the premise will still linger, shrouded in the mist of events.

Ron Hansen has authored one of the most beautiful novels of recent years, *Mariette in Ecstasy*, which has been mentioned before. It is set at the turn of the century. His heroine originally entered a convent to become a nun, was evicted for experiencing, or possibly faking, the stigmata of Christ, and generally became an outcast. He uses a particularly deft touch to end the novel [Mariette is speaking in a letter to a friend]:

> *And Christ still sends me roses. We try to be formed and held and kept by him, but instead he offers us freedom. And now when I try to know his will, his kindness floods me, his great love overwhelms me, and I hear him whisper, Surprise me.*[45]

Chapters

Throughout the novel, Hansen has walked a thin line regarding whether the woman is a fake, but his character stays true to herself to the end, and the question concerning the nature of passionate faith remains unanswered.

Steinbeck's *The Grapes of Wrath* ends on one of the strangest notes of any novel. For almost 600 pages, his characters have been driven by nature's dust storms, baked by sun in their trip across the Mojave Desert, and drenched by California rain. As the novel comes to an end, they are trapped by floodwaters in an abandoned barn. They find a man starving to death, but they have no food. The only nourishment they have is in a woman's breasts. She has just given birth to a stillborn child. The following is the novel's last paragraph:

> For a minute Rose of Sharon [the mother of the dead child] sat still in the whispering barn. Then she hoisted her tired body up and drew the comfort about her. She moved slowly to the corner and stood looking down at the wasted face [of the starving man], into the wide, frightened eyes. Then slowly she lay down beside him. He shook his head slowly from side to side. Rose of Sharon loosened one side of the blanket and bared her breast. "You got to," she said. She squirmed closer and pulled his head close. "There!" she said. "There." Her hand moved behind his head and supported it. Her fingers moved gently in his hair. She looked up and across the barn, and her lips came together and smiled mysteriously.[46]

It is as if God has made the men into children, and the young

118

mother's mysterious smile appears to be that of Mona Lisa in Leonardo da Vinci's painting, which has been the subject of so much reflection through the centuries. This startling ending causes the reader to rethink the entire novel.

SETTING AND SCENE

The first thing an author should do at the beginning of each chapter is to ground the reader in the fictional world. Work the senses. If you can hit all five in the first paragraph, you'll have your reader hooked for the entire chapter. Remember Ray Bradbury's paragraph about sensing time. Ground the reader in the unreal and establish a sense of place by choosing details that provoke emotion. Setting is environment. The author can create some of his most powerful effects by selecting the setting to augment the plotline and/or the emotional landscape inside a character. Here is Hemingway's opening to *A Farewell to Arms*:

> In the late summer of that year we lived in a house in a village that looked across the river and the plain to the mountains. In the bed of the river there were pebbles and boulders, dry and white in the sun, and the water was clear and swiftly moving and blue in the channels. Troops went by the house and down the road and the dust they raised powdered the leaves of the trees. The trunks of the trees too were dusty and the leaves fell early that year and we saw the troops marching along the road and the dust rising and leaves, stirred by the breeze, falling and the soldiers marching and afterward the road bare and white except for the leaves.[47]

By the use of natural symbolism, Hemingway's narrative gains

119

the force of a parable while spreading an atmosphere of disillusionment. All settings are exotic if they connote Premise through description, and Hemingway does this beautifully. This is narrative summary and provides the setting, but it does not constitute a scene. Four pages later, Hemingway provides his first scene:

> The priest was young and blushed easily and wore a uniform like the rest of us but with a cross in dark red velvet above the left breast pocket of his gray tunic. The captain spoke pidgin Italian for my doubtful benefit, in order that I might understand perfectly, that nothing should be lost.
>
> "Priest to-day with girls," the captain said looking at the priest and at me. The priest smiled and blushed and shook his head. This captain bated him often.
>
> "Not true?" asked the captain. "To-day I see priest with girls."
>
> "No.," said the priest. The other officers were amused at the bating.[48]

As illustrated by these paragraphs, setting describes where and when the action takes place, whereas scene describes the action. Setting may also be a metaphor for character. Since a person's home is an extension of himself, a description of the home can be a description of the person. Fitzgerald's narrator tells us that Gatsby's home:

> ...was a colossal affair by any standard—it was a factual imitation of some Hotel de Ville in Normandy, with a tower on one side, spanking new under a thin beard of raw ivy, and a marble swimming pool, and more than forty acres of lawn and

garden. It was Gatsby's mansion…[49]

The central point of course is that Gatsby's home is an "imitation" and highly pretentious. A little later at a party set inside, we learn something a little more pointed about Gatsby, who claims to be an Oxford graduate, when the narrator meets a man observing Gatsby's library:

> A stout, middle-aged man, with enormous owl-eyed spectacles, was sitting somewhat drunk on the edge of a great table, staring with unsteady concentration at the shelves of books. As we entered he wheeled excitedly around and examined Jordan from head to foot.
>
> "What do you think?" he demanded impetuously.
>
> "About what?"
>
> He waved his hand toward the book-shelves.
>
> "About that. As a matter of fact you needn't bother to ascertain. I ascertained. They're real."
>
> "The books?"
>
> He nodded.
>
> "Absolutely real—have pages and everything. I thought they'd be a nice durable cardboard. Matter of fact, they're absolutely real. Pages and—Here! Lemme show you."
>
> Taking our scepticism for granted, he rushed to the bookcases and returned with Volume One of the "Stoddard Lectures."
>
> "See!" he cried triumphantly. "It's a bona-fide piece of printed matter. It fooled me. This fella's a regular Belasco. It's a triumph. What thoroughness! What realism! Knew when to stop, too—didn't cut the pages. But what do you want? What

do you expect?"

He snatched the book from me and replaced it hastily on its shelf, muttering that if one brick was removed the whole library was liable to collapse.[50]

We then know that, although Gatsby has a large library, the books have never been read. (In those days, the edges of the pages had to be cut by hand before reading.) And in particular, the man tells us that Gatsby's life is very fragile. The narrator could have told us Gatsby was pretentious, but that wouldn't have had the impact of showing us the reality behind the façade. This also foreshadows the ending. Gatsby's nature dictates the outcome. As the story progresses, it becomes a mystery that the reader must solve. Gradually, the reader comes to realize that nothing in *The Great Gatsby* is quite what it seems, and that Fitzgerald is saying something subtle that goes beyond Gatsby, possibly something about the American Dream and the shallowness that can lie beneath a glossy surface. In the end, Gatsby's life does come tumbling down, all the subtle foreshadowing reaching fruition.

Setting may also be a reflection of internal landscape, of a character's state of mind, concerns, mood. A young, single woman with a high-paying job modeling for a prestigious agency in New York might experience the city noise as exciting, feel its energy and recognize its endless possibilities. On the other hand, a young, unemployed woman whose husband has just left her with two kids in diapers might hear the screech of tires and blasting horns as a menace, the shouts and sirens as threatening. It's all a matter of perspective, and the reader, whether the narrative is first person or third person limited, will be affected by the character through whose eyes he sees the fictional world.

Chapters

Consider this passage by Chang-Rae Lee from his novel *Native Speaker*. The first-person narrator is expressing concern for his son's safety in New York City:

> The city, of course, seemed too dangerous. Especially during the summer, the streets so dog mad with heat, untempered, literally steaming with possibilities, none of them good. People got meaner, stuck beneath all that hard light and stone. They worked through it by talking, speaking, shouting and screaming, in every language on earth. And the cursing: in New York City, summer is the season of bad language. It shouts at you from propped-up windows, it hangs on gold chains out of cars, it lingers at phone booths, peep booths, in every standing line for movies and museums and methadone.
>
> And then there were the heat waves, the crime waves. The clouds of soot and dust. In the evening it all descended unseen, an invisible ash of distant fire, soiling us everywhere.
>
> No escape.[51]

At this point, the narrator is still ruminating and grieving over the death of his son. Toward the end of the novel, however, he has reached a certain point of recovery, and it's reflected in his perception of his environment:

> Still I love it here. I love these streets lined with big American sedans and livery cars and vans. I love the early morning storefronts opening up one by one, shopkeepers talking as they crank their awnings down. I love how the Spanish disco thumps out from windows, and how the people propped halfway out still jiggle and dance in the sill and frame. I follow

the strolling Saturday families of brightly wrapped Hindus and then the black–clad Hasidim, and step into all the old churches that were once German and then Korean and are now Vietnamese. And I love the brief Queens sunlight at the end of the day, the warm lamp always reaching through the westward tops of that magnificent city.[52]

This is simply marvelous storytelling and character creation. With this scene, we can tell that Chang-Rae Lee knows his character so well that he can convey, not only his mood, but also how it affects his perception of the world. This setting has been indelibly imprinted with the character's internal state.

Again, scene differs from setting in that setting has to do with location and time, and scene has to do with a continuous action, e.g., the description of an automobile accident or a robbery. Whether a murder scene confined to an alleyway, a chase scene that circumvents a city or one that orbits an entire planet, each scene will have a setting.

Scene recreates a single incident, is continuous in time, and is action based. In this way, it differs considerably from narrative summary. All the significant events in the novel should occur within scenes. Narration during these events should be kept to a minimum and the story told through action and dialogue. See above excerpt (the second) from Hemingway's *A Farewell to Arms*. An author should deal with a scene the way a celebrity attends a party: arrive late, leave early. A chapter may consist of more than one scene, perhaps even a string of them.

PROCESSES

When creating a scene, the author should concentrate on

processes. The characters have to do something. They have lives, professions, avocations, enjoy outdoor activities, cooking, mowing the lawn, gardening. All these processes become metaphors for character. If two people fall in love in a police station, then the police station better be functioning, cops going about their business, and the reason they fall in love have something to do with the reason they are in the police station to begin with. A good example on TV is *ER*. The peoples' lives play out against the excitement of the emergency room, and the actors practice medicine as they would in real life. The processes work thematically so that they reinforce the Premise or expose an element of it along with character.

For another example of processes, consider the following from Persig's *Zen and the Art of Motorcycle Maintenance*:

> The fourth tappet *is* too loose, which is what I had hoped. I adjust it. I check the timing and see that it is still right on and the points are not pitted, so I leave them alone, screw on the valve covers, replace the plugs and start it up.[53]

Through these processes, the author brings the novel to life. This is where the novelsmith starts to gain credibility in the reader's eyes. The author must be, or appear to be, an expert in all the processes present in the novel. The reader will sense the author's confidence, or lack of it, with his material. We'll talk again about these processes and identify them when we discuss research.

TRANSITIONS BETWEEN CHAPTERS

The fire that burns in one chapter will ignite the fire that burns in the next. The beginning of a chapter is a renewal of the story, but it has its genesis in the ending of the previous chapter or at least something left unfinished. Consider the following chapter ending in Gustave Flaubert's *Madame Bovary*:

> One day as she was tidying a drawer in preparation for her departure, she pricked her finger on something sharp. It was one of the wires of her wedding bouquet. The orange-blossom was yellow with dust, the silver-trimmed satin ribbon frayed at the edges. She tossed it into the fire. It flared up like dry straw. Then it looked like a red bush burning on the embers, slowly disintegrating. She watched it burn. The little cardboard berries popped, the wire twisted, the braid melted away and the shrivelled paper petals hovered like black butterflies at the back of the fire place and finally vanished up the chimney.
>
> When they left Tostes in March, Madame Bovary was pregnant.[54]

The reader can see the state of Madame Bovary's marriage in the description of her wedding bouquet burning. This paragraph summarizes the events up to then, gives us an indication that her marriage had failed, and the last sentence, isolated to a paragraph, ignites the fire, the pregnancy, that will burn in the following chapters.

THE NOVEL AS A WEAVING

This is also a good time to stand back a little and get an overview of the way a novel is put together. Remember back to the beginning when we defined the Premise, the genetic seed of the novel, in terms of two people, or wills, in conflict. These two, the protagonist and antagonist, are like the warp and woof of an elaborate fabric. They run crossways to each other by virtue of their conflict, just as do the warp and woof. The lives of all the characters and the fictional world of the novel are superimposed as embroidery on this fabric of conflict.

The ancient Greeks used weaving, the union of opposites, as a powerful metaphor. Ancient Greek society was, to a large degree, founded upon it. Plato, in his dialogue *The Statesman,* provides a long discourse on this subject, and Scheid and Svenbro, in their book *The Craft of Zeus,* explore the significance of the weaving metaphor to both Athens and Rome.[55]

Weaving is another of the metaphors the author should carry around as he creates the novel. This is the underlying structure we have been developing. The importance of the author visualizing this cannot be overstressed because the novel is all vision, a mental creation. If no vision of its shape exists, it will have none. This process of visualization can help the author considerably to write a focused, well-balanced dream representing life.

The ancient Greeks also believed that writing was a weaving in itself. The back-and-forth placements of words on the page simulates the shuttle on its course weaving the woof threads among those of the warp. Initially, words ran both ways on the lines, as did a farmer plowing or sowing his field, and of course, as does the weaving shuttle. The Greeks believed that they had learned weaving from the spider. We can now see that setting is intimately connected with character, and character is indelibly etched in Premise, and Premise dictates plot, so that the entire novel is interlinked, and the whole must quiver when any part is touched, like an intricately woven spider web.

The problem is that, and this is what makes writing a novel an adult task, the author is never really sure of the Premise. Try as he might, certainty is rarely a part of the process. Not only that, but each character has a mind of his own and won't act in quite the way the author expects or wants. The result is that the entire novel is skewed from the author's original intention. The novel takes on a life of its own, and the author must be willing to let that happen. Frankenstein sent the electricity through the dead flesh he had assembled and screamed, "It's alive! It's alive!" only to later realize he'd created a monster he couldn't control. Just so, the novelsmith bears this same relation to his own work. It will be what it wants to be, and you should let it find its own way in the fictional world.

I've included a chapter from Melville's *Moby Dick*, Attachment III, to provide you with an example of chapter construction. I've identified all the elements, so you can relate them to what you've studied here.

THE CHAPTER BINDER

After you have created chapter summaries, put each of them in a separate compartment of a loose-leaf, three-ring binder. You'll have something on the order of twenty sections. This will bring the novel into existence. This work of the imagination will now have an identity and space in the real world. Each chapter has gained a little respect. Once it exists, the novel will seem real and not quite so large or ambiguous. You have made it into a finite entity.

Please don't brush off this suggestion. Writing a novel is a horrendous, laborious task. The novelsmith must create his book out of thin air. Nothing will make it seem more real, substantial and the task more achievable than will bringing it out of the darkness of the imagination and into the real world.

Chapters

What to put inside the binder:

1. References to pertinent material.
2. Short snippets of narrative or dialogue that come to you during the day or night, or while writing another chapter.
3. Ideas for chapter construction, setting details.
4. Interesting words, jargon.
5. Bits of dialogue.
6. All research material.

You should keep in mind that it will take you as little as two or as many as ten years to complete the novel. That's a long time. The amount of material you accumulate on each chapter will be enormous, and a binder will provide a way to organize all of it. Keep all chapter divisions even after you've written the chapter because the ideas and research material will continue to accumulate. Now, however, you will also have the text of the chapter itself in which to edit, mark up, and take notes.

Remember that nothing in this structural approach is independent of your own basic idea for the novel. Yours is the metal put into the smithy's fire. You heat it, beat it into shape using this structure, but the initial impulse and all the material of the novel come from your own idea. The approach provided here is the smithy, the hammer and anvil, and only shapes it.

EXERCISES
(a) Provide a detailed chapter list along with a one-sentence statement of the each chapter's central point. (b) Describe how each chapter advances the storyline and relate it to the overall novel geometry. (c) Provide a list of the major processes to be exploited.

CHAPTER 9: Research

First of all, research isn't something you do once for a few days before getting on with the business of writing. It's an ongoing process, with little letup until the novel is finished. When you write, you write "in the moment," and you need all your accumulated knowledge at hand to create the reality. What you don't need is the uncertainty of a poorly researched fictional world. Research and planning allow you to release yourself from holding the world in place, so you can allow your characters to surprise you with their inherent spontaneity and inventiveness as you write.

Premise, structure and characterization are the blood, bones and flesh of the novel, and narration is the bolt of lightning that gives it life, as Mary Shelly's Frankenstein gave life to his monster. Research, then, becomes the nourishment to sustain life. It gives the novel authenticity. It is the food, drink, vitamins, and emotional nourishment that give it strength and health. As this literary being grows from conception through childhood to maturity, it needs nourishment and medication for its ills. It needs encouragement. All that nurturing comes from research. Just as sunshine and rain come from above and give life to all that grows, and the Earth provides nourishment from below to sustain it, so research comes from both above and below, as illustrated in Figure 13.

Research

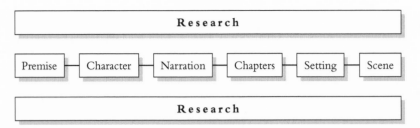

Figure 13

Research should be targeted at specifics. Know what element of your novel you are researching. But due to serendipity, you may pick up along the way all sorts of interesting tidbits to enhance other aspects. All research is ultimately directed at creating verisimilitude, i.e., having the quality of truth, being probable. The reader can't suspend disbelief if the world of the novel is not developed so that each element in it appears authentic.

But, what to research? As with every question concerning your novel, always return to Premise to find the answer.

RESEARCHING PREMISE

Remember that premise may exist on three levels. For example:

1. Cosmic Premise (good overcomes evil). The novel's deepest level.
2. Story Premise (freedom overcomes bondage)
3. Character Premise (self-reliance overcomes arrogance)

Each of these levels contains three elements: the two forces opposing each other and the conflict that connects them. You must research the philosophical ideas inherent in each of these. Even a dictionary definition can set you on the right course and provide necessary insight to help construct a storyline or character. The above Premise elements are defined as follows:[56]

Good: Something conforming to the moral order of the universe. Praiseworthy. Having intrinsic value. Favored or preferred.

Evil: Morally reprehensible, sinful. Causing discomfort or repulsion. Offensive, disagreeable. Something bringing sorrow, distress, or calamity, suffering, misfortune.

Freedom: The absence of necessity, coercion, or constraint in choice or action. Liberation from slavery or restraint or from the power of another. Independence. The power of acting without compulsion. Not being unduly hampered or frustrated.

Bondage: The state of being bound by compulsion. Captivity, serfdom, servitude or subjugation to a controlling person.

Self-reliance: Reliance on one's own efforts and abilities, powers or judgment.

Arrogance: A feeling of superiority manifested in an overbearing manner or presumptuous claims. Exaggerating or disposed to exaggerate one's own worth or importance in an overbearing manner. Overly proud.

Even after just ten minutes with a dictionary, you can begin to see useful characteristics unfolding. Further research might include reading mythology and religion to get the cosmic elements, history to get story elements, and biographies to get character elements.

Research

RESEARCHING CONFLICT

Conflict has two basic components: (1) the struggle over the solution to a problem and (2) the egotistical struggle for power. Frequently power issues will overshadow the problem that brings the two characters into conflict. Don't allow this to happen without being conscious of it. Pure ego struggles have limited insight and become stereotypically easily to dramatize because of the limited anguish of choice.

Conflict, which is based on different philosophies concerning the nature of a problem, has a transcendent quality in resolution. This occurs when people engage each other in highly emotional dialogue or negotiation. Neither side backs off but engages the opposition in a process of "talking the subject to pieces." The process may, but not necessarily, become violent. The process is then one of consciousness raising, although both parties may not see the light, or perhaps neither will, but the reader will. This process throws light into the depths of darkness, but also allows one to experience the most profound insights of which they are capable.

Some experts claim that the Premise behind all stories can be reduced to good versus evil. This may be so, and at the cosmic level, this is fine. But carrying that pure element of goodness or evilness into the characters leaves them without any real human depth. This results in stereotypical characters that are uninteresting. Always provide a human depth to your characters, particularly your protagonist and antagonist. You do this by providing the characters with vulnerability. This elevates the story philosophically.

You may be in tune with one side or the other of a conflict (this prejudice is generally reflected in the Premise), and this prejudice may not permit you to thoroughly develop the "orphaned" viewpoint. To help round out the arguments, you need to research each side thoroughly.

RESEARCHING STORYLINE

Research can actually be the first step in getting an idea for a novel. If an author wants to write a novel but doesn't really have an idea, he should follow his interests. If he likes sunsets, he could start by researching sunsets, and then he might settle on an idea for a novel about a photographer who photographs sunsets. Sunsets, the close of day, are symbolic of endings, but also of the denizens of the dark, owls, and all things hidden and secretive. The author might wonder what the photographer's secret is and turn to biographies of famous photographers.

If you're interested in writing a modern rendition of an ancient storyline, an excellent source is Edward Tripp's *The Meridian Handbook of Classical Mythology*. He provides not only the storylines but also the sources of the ancient texts. This is by far the best handbook of Greek mythology in or out of print. There is nothing quite like it.

RESEARCHING CHARACTER

Research personalities, human behavior (be careful with this, no psychobabble), processes, professions, philosophy, dialects. Research your thematic character's special wisdom. Perhaps he is an astronomer or a hobo, both of which would require extensive research. Use process to expose culture and character.

Some authors use mythological characters as models. Jean Shinoda Bolen's *Gods in Everyman* and *Goddesses in Everywoman* describe the archetypes of human personality represented by the ancient Greek gods. Bolen provides the following discussion of the Greek fire god, Hephaestus:

> The fire associated with Hephaestus is fire under the earth that molten core that rises from the depths as the lava of volcanoes. Subterranean fire is a metaphor for passionate feelings: intense sexual and erotic fire contained within the body until it is expressed, or rage and anger that is held in and dampened down, or a passion for beauty that is stirring and felt in the body (or earth of the person).
>
> These feelings, which lie beneath the surface in a deeply introverted person, may suddenly and unexpectedly erupt. When revealed to another person in a moment of intimate conversation, almost invariably that person is surprised; "I had no idea that you felt this strongly."[57]

Hephaestus was also deformed at birth, his feet turned front to back, which gave his gait a forward rolling motion. This deformity could also be viewed as an emotional crippling, and the god's abnormal gait would translate into some hypersensitivity. Using this method to generate character, allows you to get your foot in the door. Generating character from nothing is a difficult task, and pulling open that door to a room full of perceptions just might jumpstart your imagination.

Bolen provides a shopping list of personality traits from which the author may select. Using this type of research to develop characters should never be done arbitrarily, but always under the influence of the Premise, and only to gain further insight into a developing character or trigger the creative process.

The ancient Greek, Theophrastus (370-287 BC), provided a

short set of stereotypes (thirty in all) still helpful today in his book that has come to be called *Characters*. The following excerpts illustrate his keen sensitivity and are a veritable smorgasbord of personal shortcomings:

> The garrulous man is the sort who says to anyone he meets that he is talking nonsense—no matter what that man may tell him—and that he knows it all himself, and if he listens, he'll find out about it. And as the other tries to answer, he keeps interrupting and says, "Now don't forget what you intend to say!"
>
> ---
>
> The superstitious man is the sort who washes his hands, sprinkles himself with water from a shrine, puts a sprig of laurel in his mouth and walks around that way all day. If a weasel crosses his path he goes no further until someone passes between them, or he throws three stones over the road.[58]

A novelsmith could do worse than decide to add one of these attributes to a character in his novel.

Use physical landscape as a metaphor for internal landscape. Pick up a National Geographic book on one of the national parks, the Grand Canyon for example. Use the photographs, not literally, but metaphorically. One can well imagine the void left in a man after his wife's death as the Grand Canyon of the soul, parts of it so deeply cut by pain that the mid-summer sun could cast little more than a dark shadow across it. View the physical world as internal landscape, mood.

Using the characteristics of animals to describe someone can also capture their physical, or even emotional, essence. Consider

Research

this description of a woman from James Salter's highly-acclaimed *Light Years*:

> She is dressed in her oat-colored sweater, slim as a pike, her long hair fastened, the fire crackling. Her real concern is the heart of existence: meals, bed linen, clothing. The rest means nothing; it is managed somehow. She has a wide mouth, the mouth of an actress, thrilling, bright. Dark smudges in her armpits, mint on her breath. Her nature is extravagant. She buys on impulse, she visits Bendel's as she would a friend's, collects dirty clothes. She is twenty-eight. Her dreams still cling to her, adorn her; she is confident, composed, she is related to long-necked creatures, ruminants, abandoned saints. She is careful, hard to approach. Her life is concealed. It is through the smoke and conversation of many dinners that one sees her...[59]

Her hair is like "fire crackling," and Salter compares her to a pike (a large elongated, long-snouted fish valued for food and sport), long-necked creatures (cranes and ostriches come to mind), and then a ruminant (an even-toed, hoofed mammal that chews its cud). The point is that you should research description and pursue every avenue in creating your vision of the character. Pull on every source imaginable to stimulate your imagination so you can stimulate your reader's.

When researching character, the author should remember that his characters are inexorably attached to premise, and that the heart of the character (along with his strength and weakness) is inherent in it.

Research

RESEARCHING THE SENSES

While researching other elements of your novel, research the senses. This is a first priority because the senses center the reader in the fictional world. Concentrate your research on the three "forgotten" ones because they work on the subconscious. (Remember Ray Bradbury's description of Mars: What is the smell, taste and touch of the time?) Here, the writer develops a strategy for using them because they season the narrative as spices do food. You don't season fried chicken the same as you do chicken cacciatore. Too much and you'll overwhelm the reader, but just the right sense at the proper moment catapults the reader to a new level of awareness.

Where do you go to research the senses? The primary source is the real world. Visit the places where your story takes place, or find similar settings. And while there, close your eyes, stick your fingers in your ears and smell, taste and touch your surroundings. Eat in the restaurants. Walk the parks, smell the trees, chew a blade of grass.

Secondary sources include books (cookbooks, flower books, the encyclopaedia will sometimes tell how things smell or feel). Medical books give strange odors that come with disease. Also remember that you don't have to be literal. Things smell like other things: "Tom's breath was like a rotting carcass." You can use smells, tastes and tactile sensations symbolically and metaphorically. You can say things like, "Tom's personality was so grating that just looking at him felt like sand in the teeth."

RESEARCHING SETTING

Use travel guides and nature books to get the flora and fauna. Use city, state, and country histories (you can't know a place without knowing what it's been through). Remember that setting is also a reflection of character internal landscape. Once you determine the literal part of the setting, take it that further step and "color" it with the character's mood. To research mood, pickup a good psychology book.

RESEARCHING SCENE

As described in the chapter on chapters, a scene has to do with a dramatized action, and must involve conflict on some level. Sometimes you'll know precisely how to dramatize a scene, but when intuition fails, go to other authors you admire to see how they do it.

RESEARCHING PROCESSES

Interview professionals: lawyers, policemen, forensic experts, bakers, clergy, etc. Also don't forget housewives, mothers, fathers, CEO's, ditch diggers, gravediggers, etc. Even kids have a particular slant on the world that might be crucial in some novels. In Carlsbad, New Mexico, the potash mines are an exotic setting that could be used in a novel, and the mining process would be a fascinating backdrop. The Carlsbad Caverns have a metaphoric appeal that could be exploited. A story about a seagull would require that the author research flying. Richard Bach (*Jonathan Livingston Seagull*) was a pilot.

STRANGE WORLD WE LIVE IN

The world of the novel and the real world are different places. Dialogue sounds different, descriptions fall flat, and the lives of characters demand a sense of story. Fiction can never match the strangeness of real life. It has been said that fiction has to conform to what is possible, real life doesn't. This is the constraint the storyteller is always trying to overcome. In *Groundhog Day*, we find a story where the impossible works perfectly, a single day repeating thousands of times.

We think of the world as commonplace. It is anything but. Before 9/11, few would have thought that they'd wake up one morning and the World Trade Center would be on fire, but absolutely no one would have believed that two hours later both towers would be in rubble.

The author must always look for the strange element in his novel. You can't make it strange enough. Your characters can't be off-the-wall enough. As another example, who would believe that a seventeen-year-old peasant girl could take over as commander in chief of a country's army? In two years, she would win a war that had been going on for 100. Joan of Arc did it for France. When the English captured her, the French wouldn't negotiate for her return and allowed the English to burn her at the stake.

KEEPING AT IT

The author should not assume that once he has described a character, either internally or externally, or a setting, that the job is complete. Every time the reader comes into contact with the character or place, they should be subjected to an ever deepening, evolving personality and presence. The author continues to research his characters and setting to develop new ideas about these people and the places they inhabit.

THE MULTI-MIND PRINCIPLE

James Cameron has said that the reason movies are such a powerful medium is that they are, by their very nature, collaborative. By extensive, even exhaustive, research, a writer can also bring other minds to bear on his work. This will give it that "three-dimensional" feel achieved by collaboration.

RESEARCH RESOURCES

Visit the actual physical sites in which your novel's scenes take place. Visit local libraries, and investigate, not only books, but also CDs and DVDs about your location. On the Internet, most towns and organizations now have websites. Amazon.com claims to be the largest bookstore in the world. It contains millions of titles. The Advanced Book Exchange, abe.com, is the world's largest source for out-of-print books. Also Google has scanned many out-of-print books and presents them online where you can search their contents.

Perhaps your most valued resource will be Wikipedia. It is the largest encyclopedia in existence and is still growing. However, volunteers have put together Wikipedia, and you must always cast a suspicious eye toward any factual material you find there. Still, it's a marvelous place to start your research

THE RESEARCH PLAN

The Research Plan contains sources for researching the following:

- Premise
- The Nature of Conflict
- Character
- The Underside of Your Characters
- Strengths and Weaknesses
- Narration

Research

- POV
- Voice
- Tense
- Chapters
- Transitions
- First and Last Chapters
- Creating scenes
- Processes
- Setting
- Language
- Narrative voice
- Speech (dialogue)
- The Senses

Once you have addressed all these topics, you can approach your novel with confidence. You will still have questions as you proceed with the writing of it, but these questions will be at the second level and will not work on your confidence that you can actually accomplish this enormous task you've undertaken.

EXERCISES
(a) Write a Research Plan. (b) Provide a list of sources you plan to consult to research the novel, where you plan to go and what you expect to get from each. (c) Perform the initial research on the Premise and write one page expounding upon it. (d) Now is the time to start writing a two-to-three paragraph summary of each chapter.

CHAPTER 10: The Psychology of Creativity

Now that we've explored novel structure, its constituents, and its connection to the external world through research, we'll explore its relationship to the novelsmith's internal world. The author creates the novel within his psychic landscape, and to study this process, we must delve deeply into psychology. This is the creative process in detail, its mysticism. Since storytelling is, in its essence, myth, we will rely heavily on Jungian psychology.

One might view the creation of the novel as coming solely from two places: the external world and the novelsmith's internal world, neither of which should be neglected when studying craft. The dual flow of information into the novel can be graphically depicted as in Figure 14:

Information Flow

Figure 14

We have a tendency to envision the external, physical world as "real" and the internal as imaginary, or "unreal." Thus, we may neglect the imaginary in favor of the real. To get a good grasp of his creative process, the author must develop the tools to deal with his internal processes, which in large part go unnoticed. Initially, we will take a look at the external world and, to a certain extent, "discredit" it. It is not as "real" as you might think. Following this, we will explore the credibility of the other world, the internal, to provide a more balanced picture of the human landscape. The result may dispel your concrete belief in the literal world and elevate your estimation of the non-literal one.

THE NATURE OF REALITY

In the opening chapter, we talked about novelsmithing as a process of both method and madness. So far, we've dealt only with method. We also talked about how storytelling comes down to us as an art thousands of years old, from ancient myth-making. For Western Civilization, the writing of stories on papyrus goes back to Homer in 750 BC, but the oldest surviving story ever written is the *Epic of Gilgamesh,* which was recorded on clay tablets around 2700 BC. The story was undoubtedly much older than the tablets discovered by archaeologists, because it was the result of an oral tradition in which stories were passed down from generation to generation. Apparently, storytelling is just a part of the human endeavor. To fully understand the nature of storytelling, we'll have to understand a little more about our own psychology and how we create reality.

What we call the real world is a figment of our imagination. Nothing on earth or in the heavens is solid. Matter itself is composed of atoms, which are 99+% vacuum. Matter also has both particle and wave manifestations, and thus is ephemeral in its very nature. Quantum theory tells us that even the way matter is put together is uncertain, with particles having only a statistically probable presence. Physicists tell us that the world is built from our senses. The Nobel laureate Erwin Schroedinger put it this way:

> ...the stuff from which our world picture is built was yielded exclusively from the sense organs as organs of the mind, so that every man's world picture is and always remains a construct of his mind and cannot be proved to have any other existence...[60]

Psychologists also tell us that the universe really exists only as we know it in our own minds. We "create" the universe with information received from our five senses. Even our most powerful sense, sight, gives us a false representation of the world. We believe we see an object, but in fact we only see light reflected from it. Our brains are accustomed to, and specifically built for, decoding the characteristics of light, and from it we create our vision of the world. The senses of touch and hearing also play a powerful role in our formulation of the world, smell and taste more minor ones. A close-knit relationship exists between what is "out there" and what "resides within" because the one holds the key to our understanding of the other. The key to decoding the universe is within ourselves. We inherit the key, or at least humanity's vision of it.

This is only the first level of "false" reality. Tables, chairs, roads, cars, our entire culture, is a construct of the human mind. They are objects in the "real" world, but only serve our perception of what they are. They are a result of culture. An alien race of beings would have no idea of these objects' use any more than if they were rocks on a beach. So, the fact that an object is a chair resides within us and not within the chair, yet we think of the lump of wood as a chair without question. Culture comes from within the human psyche and is projected onto the external world.

Books and writing are a further level of human creation. The words on a page only make sense to someone versed in their learning and practiced in their interpretation. In a very real sense, they only reorder what is already within us. They have no content other than to those who can read meaning into them. Even news stories taken from our own lives are mental constructs, human invention. They are not even summaries, but constructions pieced together from parts of a much richer experience. We learn to use story as the conduit of communication. Our lives contain no stories. Biography and history are the invention of the mind. History didn't exist until the 5th century BC, when Herodotus wrote about the Persian invasion. All of these constructs result from the nature of human consciousness. We tend to live our lives and interpret our memories of them in terms of story. We single out the facts that fit into story based on what we interpret as significant. The introduction of these concepts is not meant to trivialize reality, but to call to your attention to how we construct "reality."

Where does that leave us relative to the novel? We can see that our minds are not strangers to the "creation" process. When a reader picks up a novel, he already possesses all the skills necessary to imagine the world created within the book. He is now and always has been creating, imagining, the real world with data from the five senses. While reading a novel, though, the stimulus doesn't come from the outside world. The reader's imagination is stimulated by the author's words. It bears restatement: When a reader picks up a novel, he enters a world in which he suffers total sensory deprivation. We know from deprivation experiments that without outside stimulus, the mind has a tendency to hallucinate,[61] and since some part of the reader must reside within the fictional world, a world of total sensory deprivation, the potential for hallucination exists.

We've all experienced this "creative" act before. When we look at a pattern in the grain of a rock, our minds tend to create an image, e.g., a man on horseback, or a ship at sea. This is projection. We project some image contained within us onto an external object. This is also, however, a creative act, perhaps *the* creative act.

Psychologists use this ability with the irregular, random shape of the Rorschach inkblot to determine a patient's mental state. This is a natural tendency of the human mind. We're at it all the time, creating reality. Using this same technique, the mind can invent a complete story from only a few facts. Just as the mind "imagines" the external world using the stimulus of the senses, the reader, by starting with only the seed of an idea created by words on the page, dips into his own imagination to invent, to create, the world present in the novel. Every reader has a unique version of what he reads and creates a unique fictional world. That's the reason some will like a certain novel and others detest it. This creates terrific problems when critiquing a work, a topic for discussion in Chapter 12.

A novel is little more than a "blueprint" for constructing a particular fictional world. This is the reason that good readers are as important as good writers. They have to know how to decode the words on the page and create the fictional dream within themselves. The novelsmith, he who writes the words, goes a step deeper into his own imagination than does a reader into his. The author doesn't even have the stimulus of the words, but must suck the story from his own imagination. This is not an easy process.

The Psychology of Creativity

Writers suffer from distractions, writer's block, and generally just grumble a lot.

Why is writing so difficult? What is this internal process? Why do some writers say that, while writing, they exist in a state of total terror? We might rephrase these questions: What is the nature of our imagination? From where do we retrieve the information that we put into a novel? What is the source of creativity? What is the material of the imagination?

We will answer these questions one by one, but first we need to build a little background concerning the human psyche.

The answers lie in the relationship between psychology and art. To understand this relationship, we'll turn to Carl Jung. From him we'll learn that this invented, fictional world is not so much a lie as it might first appear. Much of what follows has been also influenced by *Jung's Map of the Soul* by Murray Stein, which is a brilliant summary of Jung's thoughts on the subject.

JUNG'S VIEW OF THE HUMAN PSYCHE

Carl Jung was the father of what is known as analytical psychology, so called because its principles are derived from experimentation. Jung was a Swiss-born psychologist and psychiatrist, and a student and collaborator of Sigmund Freud for several years until they had a falling-out, after which Jung founded his own school in Zurich. Jung placed emphasis on "the will to live" whereas Freud placed it on "the sex drive."

THE EGO

Jung's view of the psyche begins with the ego, the consciousness that forms the center of self-awareness. The ego, what we refer to when we say, "I" or "me," is the mirror in which the psyche sees itself. It is not the entire consciousness, but simply an agent of the psyche, a focus of consciousness, and the center of awareness. The ego is a part of a greater psychic entity, the self. The ego provides freewill, yet it is morally neutral. It feels as if it has existed forever.

THE PERSONA

The core of the ego doesn't change over the life of the individual, but during childhood, culture creates a layer around its center called the "persona." The persona constitutes that portion of the ego acceptable to the outside world. The persona is a societal mask that makes a favorable impression on others and conceals, hides, our more base instincts.

This seems to be a really good situation. As the child grows, his persona develops, and he learns how to deal with his culture and becomes a nice person by projecting his persona. But the development of the persona has consequences because the ego, self-centered as it is, isn't so eager to give up these other qualities that aren't so socially and culturally acceptable. These negative qualities aren't just eliminated and have to go somewhere.

THE SHADOW

That rejected, suppressed part of the ego no longer forms a part of consciousness and becomes the ego's shadow, which is immoral or at least disreputable within the culture. Rather ominously, the shadow retains elements of freewill and decision-making. Most of us are unaware of our shadow, so that it is not fully under control. Thus, this "bad-guy" shadow constitutes an opposite for the "good-guy" persona. As you can well imagine, the relationship between the persona and the shadow is the source of much

The Psychology of Creativity

internal conflict.

Remember that we are investigating the novelsmith's psyche; however, this preliminary information may be of some help to the novelsmith in developing characters. It might help him round out a character that he can't seem to get to come to life. But he should not overuse this knowledge. Make sure you don't deconstruct your character with psychobabble.

Now, on with our investigation of the novelsmith's source of creativity.

THE UNCONSCIOUS

The shadow is not the entire unconscious. The unconscious is that part of the individual's psyche that is unknown to the person and includes the vast bulk of the psychic world. During a child's development, the conscious ego is subjected to disturbances from the external world. These "collisions" between the ego and the world can be positive, in that they stimulate ego development in the directions of stronger problem solving and autonomy, and the results remain in the conscious part of the psyche. But they also can be negative if the disturbances are too traumatizing.

Collisions also occur between the ego and "objects" occupying the vast unconscious psychic space. Jung termed these unconscious objects, "complexes." Complexes are psychic entities outside consciousness that cause ego disturbances from within the individual. They constitute the contents of the unconscious. These complexes are our inner demons. They come upon us from within and catch us by surprise. These complexes are what generate nightmares. Children intuitively detect and fear this internal psychic space.

This is shown diagrammatically in Figure 15:

The Psychology of Creativity

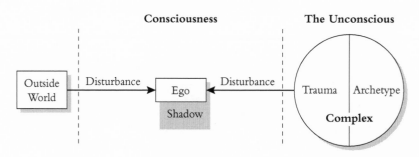

Figure 15

One might well imagine this hidden internal landscape to be, metaphorically, the Labyrinth of Greek myth. If we choose to encounter this part of ourselves, we must descend into the Labyrinth, as did Theseus, paying out Ariadne's tread to help us find our way back. At the end of the Labyrinth, we'll find the Minotaur, the half-man, half-animal part of ourselves we recognize as "the other."

Each complex is dual, consisting of the pairing of an image produced by trauma, and an innate archetypal component closely related to it. Trauma is the creating force behind complexes. Prior to trauma, the archetypal object exists as an image and a motivating force, but does not have the anxiety-producing quality of the complex. Trauma provides the emotionally charged memory that becomes associated with the archetypal image, the two welding in the processes. The complex then becomes enriched by similar experiences. Complexes are so emotionally laden that they can erupt spontaneously into consciousness and take possession of the ego. We are rarely aware this is happening. The ego is deceived into believing it is acting autonomously.

The Psychology of Creativity

The part of the complex caused by trauma is personal and composed of forgotten and repressed personal experience. This forms what Jung called the "personal unconscious." The other part of the complex contains the primitive archetypal component and is termed the "collective unconscious." Each complex is an image, and images are the essence of the psyche. Dreams are formed of these unconscious images and behave as a stranger in the sphere of consciousness. When activated, a complex makes us feel as though we are in the grip of an alien entity. As might be expected, the archetypal images of the mother and father are the giants of the unconscious.

Human beings are not blank slates when born. Archetypal components are inherited and not acquired. They belong to us by virtue of being human and are not derived from culture. Culture is derived from them. And this is really the operative statement for the novelsmith. These archetypal images are the cornerstone of our imaginative craft, along with, of course, the way they function within the psyche.

THE COLLECTIVE UNCONSCIOUS

The deepest layer of the psyche is the collective unconscious. It is a combination of universally prevalent patterns and forces, "archetypes" and "instincts," that constitute nature's gift to each of us. Jung put it this way:

> Man "possesses" many things which he has never acquired but has inherited from his ancestors. ... he brings with him systems that are organized and ready to function in a specifically human way, and these he owes to millions of years of human development. Just as the migratory and nest-building

instincts of birds were never learnt or acquired individually, man brings with him at birth the ground-plan of his nature, and not only of his individual nature but of his collective nature. These inherited systems correspond to the human situations that have existed since primeval times: youth and old age, birth and death, sons and daughters, father and mothers, mating, and so on. Only the individual consciousness experiences these things for the first time, but not the bodily system and the unconscious. For them they are only the habitual functioning of instinct that were preformed long ago.[62]

For a writer, the most important fact about the collective unconscious is the inherited archetypal images. They attract the psychic energy and are the origin of culture.

... the archetype appears in the form of a spirit in dreams or fantasy products, or even comports itself like a ghost. There is a mystical aura about its numinosity, and it has a corresponding effect upon the emotions. It mobilizes philosophical and religious convictions in the very people who deemed themselves miles above any such fit of weakness. Often it drives with unexampled passion and remorseless logic towards its goal and draws the subject under its spell, from which despite the most desperate resistance he is unable, and finally no longer even willing, to break free, because the experience brings with it a depth of fullness of meaning that was unthinkable before.[63]

These "fantasy products" are the material of the artistic imagination. Archetypal images are beyond direct human grasp and form a realm of the psyche. However, they are somewhat accessible. Standing before this realm of the collective unconscious is a "presence" called the "anima" in men and the "animus" in women. The anima/us provides access to the archetypal images. The anima/us is the mechanism that energizes the author's imagination.

THE PERSONA AND ANIMA/US BRIDGES

Just as the persona provides a protective bridge between the ego and the outside world, the anima/us bridges the ego and the collective unconscious. See figure 16.

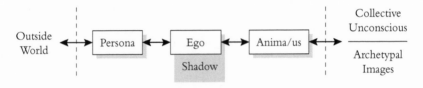

Figure 16

The persona faces outward, into the social world and assists with necessary external adaptations. Similarly, the anima/us faces inward, toward the inner realm and helps adapt to thoughts, feelings, images, and emotions confronting the ego from this internal source. In men, the anima tends to be a feminine presence and hypersensitive, dripping with sentimentality. In women, the animus tends to have the emotional energy of an opinionated bully. As Murray Stein puts it: "Men in the grip of the anima tend to withdraw into hurt feelings, and women in the grip of the animus tend to attack."[64]

Although at first, it might seem a contradiction that men essentially have a feminine personality standing at the gate to their collective unconscious and women a masculine one, but it re-

154

sults from the processes of conception. When a boy is conceived, the masculine elements are liberated and feminine elements shut down to become the hidden anima. For a girl, the feminine elements are liberated and masculine elements shut down to become the hidden animus. However, the influence of the anima/us, particularly when it's not integrated with the ego, is so profound that it can dominate the personality. As human beings, we tend to project everything that is not integrated and remains unconscious. As long as the anima/us is unconscious, it becomes a projected perception of the outside world.

In one of its most powerful manifestations, the anima/us is the ever-receding mirage of the eternal beloved. A man then chooses as his lover, the woman who best fits his own unconscious femininity, i.e., she who can receive the projection of the feminine presence standing before his collective unconscious. A woman chooses as her lover, the man who best fits her own unconscious masculinity.

Murray Stein describes the ideally developed person:

> The conscious and unconscious parts of the psychic system work together in a balanced and harmonious interplay, and this takes place in part between the anima/us and the persona. Here the ego is not flooded by material from without or within but is rather facilitated and protected by these structures. ... The persona is able to adapt to the demands of life and to manage stable relations with the surrounding social and natural worlds. Internally there is well managed and steady access to a wellspring of energy and creative inspiration. Outer and inner adaptations are adequate to the demands of life.[65]

The Psychology of Creativity

The reason most of us rarely experience life like this is that we pay no attention to our inner development. We don't teach the mechanics of how to do this in our schools and even ostracize those who seek help when overcome by internal turmoil. Most of us are primitive internally. We act as if we have no need to understand ourselves and blame our problems on the external world, when most psychological problems have internal causes. Too bad we don't get a *User's Manual for the Psyche* when we're born.

Now here comes the most exciting part for the writer, and this is the reason we have labored over understanding all this Jungian psychology. For the novelsmith, this is the internal point of contact between the author and the material he is shaping, where the hammer strikes the metal: the interaction between the ego and the anima/us is essentially one of conflict and confrontation. If this is beginning to sound like the cauldron wherein the Premise is born, you are getting the message. The ego engages the anima/us in a process of head-to-head confrontation during which differences become differentiated and articulated.

The ancient Greeks had a term for this anima/us: the muse. The muse has come down to us as a personage that provides the novelsmith with his inspired material. At the beginning of *The Odyssey*, when Homer says, "Sing in me, Muse, and through me tell the story..." he is consciously calling to his anima. The anima/us, our muse, provides a guiding influence through the archetypal images that are within the collective unconscious and, therefore, beyond ourselves. Eventually, clarity is achieved in the conflict we have created, and therefore, the process, deeply steeped in conflict, becomes one of consciousness raising. The process has allowed the novelsmith to experience the profound heights and depths of one's own mental universe and return transformed.

TRANSCENDENCE THROUGH CONFLICT

Perhaps we can now understand why fiction is so heavily dependent on conflict, and why the Premise, the DNA of storytelling, is the cornerstone of the novel. The characters in a novel are engaged in the same conflict/resolution process as that in which the ego and the anima/us are engaged. We can further understand why we require that a novel have meaning. We expect a work of fiction to do more than just help us escape our worldly dilemmas. We expect it to have importance and be meaningful. A story is a process of discovery-through-conflict, and that process must result in transcendence for the central character. He must be changed by the experience, thereby allowing the reader to also be changed.

A novel is a reflection of the life process, the conflict/resolution process in which the ego and anima/us engage. Creating a novel brings that process into the imagination where it can be experienced. This is the work of consciousness raising, and the reason Premise has a cosmic quality that adds spiritual depth to the work. The reason fiction exists at all is that it is the mechanism that gives expression to the conflict between the ego and the anima/us and allows it into consciousness. All stories have meaning and are morally directed, either consciously or unconsciously, because the ego-anima/us conflict is morally based.

Not only is this the reason Premise works, but it also explains why the Premise is so difficult to grasp in our own work and see in others'. It constitutes the novel's unconscious, the unseen structure underlying its basic motivation.

The fact that every author has an anima/us may very well be the reason women can write good male characters and men can write good female characters. The image of the other sex is already buried within us. The reason we can develop such a variety of characters is that the anima/us is so complex. A comment by Jung illustrates the diversity of a man's anima:

> ...the anima is bipolar and can therefore appear positive one moment and negative the next; now young, now old; now mother, now maiden; now a good fairy, now a witch; now a saint, now a whore. Besides this ambivalence, the anima also has "occult" connections with "mysteries," with the world of darkness in general, and for that reason she often has a religious tinge. ...as a rule she is more or less immortal, because [she resides] outside time.[66]

Murray Stein describes the animus:

> ...a woman with an "animus problem" is also overcome by her unconscious, typically by emotionally charged thoughts and opinions which control her more than she controls them. ... These autonomous ideas and opinions end up disturbing her adaptation to the world because they are delivered with the emotional energy of a bully. Often they wreak havoc on her relationship, because the people near her must build self-protective shields around themselves when they are with her. They feel on the defensive and uncomfortable in her presence. Hard as she may want to be receptive and intimate, she cannot because her ego is subject to these invasions of disruptive energies that transform her into anything but a kinder, gentler person she would like to be. Instead, she is abrasive and gripped by unconscious strivings for power and control.[67]

The Psychology of Creativity

These then are the central figures, the internal ghosts, that reek havoc in our lives. And it is through them that the novel-smith must receive his creative impulses. Let's take the study of the archetype one step further, and then we will have pretty much exhausted the subject as it applies to the author. Another branch of Jungian psychology comes into play.

ARCHETYPAL PSYCHOLOGY

Archetypal psychology, as an outgrowth of Jungian theory, is affiliated with the arts and culture.[68] As archetypal psychologists view it, the archetype, as a part of the collective unconscious, is accessible to the imagination and presents itself as an image. The image is not viewed as a mental construct, but as the basic unit of the psyche; therefore, it is irreducible. Archetypes are the fundamental patterns of existence. These archetypal images come and go of their own will and are transcendent to the world of sense. Archetypes are viewed as the primary forms that govern the psyche, and thus, archetypal psychology is linked with culture and the imagination, rather than the medical and empirical psychologies of Freud and Jung. According to James Hillman, the originator of archetypal psychology:

> The primary, and irreducible, language of these archetypal patterns is the metaphorical discourse of myths. These therefore can be understood as the most fundamental patterns of human existence.[69]

This is of crucial importance to the novelsmith because to glimpse an imagined reality, which is exactly what he does during the creation of stories that are all actually myths, requires methods and perceptual faculties different from those used to see the sensual world. The writer must become sensitive to the imagined realities emanating from the collective unconscious and develop the skills to handle them. These skills come with practice, and we do it by paying close attention to the psychology of our characters. We learn to read their motivations and put them on the printed page.

With this new knowledge of the novelsmith's toolbox, mythology takes on a much heavier significance. These stories, which have come down to us through the millennia, have been on the anvil many times, being heated, scraped and pounded until they have merged repeatedly and separated again and again from the reality that spawned them until they became amalgams and alloys. They form "composite" stories we hear so much about that have become the story of Abraham and Isaac, that of Oedipus, and King David. They tell us something profound about human existence. As Thornton Wilder put it:

> ...myth-making is one of the means whereby the generalized truths of human knowledge finds expression and particularly the disavowed impulses of the mind escape the 'censor' of acquired social control and find their way into indirect confession. Myths constitute the dreaming subconscious soul of the race telling its story.[70]

We can see then that the process of novelsmithing is not so much one of fabricating a false reality, as it is one of discovering a mythology, one that may be highly personal and at the same time of universal significance. The personal nature of it comes from the fact that the complexes of the personal unconscious are formed through trauma colliding with an archetype. As we stated earlier, "trauma provides the emotionally charged memory that becomes associated with the archetypal image, the two welding in the processes."

We can also see why the novelsmith will frequently take on the neuroses of his characters. It is because he is experiencing the trauma, one might even say creating the trauma. The novelsmith can't escape it because it occurs inside him, and he is not simply witnessing an external event.

We don't have a set of instructions that tell us how to develop these inspirational skills; however, we can note that dreams and states near sleep seem to put us particularly close to the source of inspiration, this collective unconscious. Thus, we come to the psychic state known as liminality.

LIMINALITY

Without a set of instructions for courting and dealing with inspiration, it might be thought that the best the novelsmith can do is to put himself in a position to experience it and wait for it to happen. He sits down before his word processor, takes a sip of coffee, places his hands on the keyboard, and waits. However, his muse, his anima, may have turned her back on him.

If this happens, he can go a little further still toward getting her attention through a concept called "liminality." The word "liminal" means "threshold," "entrance." Liminality is the threshold of conscious awareness, the twilight zone between the waking and sleeping states, the conscious and the unconscious. Another characteristic of this state is that our identity is held in suspension. We are no longer fixed in our perception of others or ourselves. This is an ideal state for the novelsmith because he is then free to

161

assume another identity and perceive the world in ways he could never imagine otherwise.

The question then becomes: how to access information beyond this threshold, how to entice it across by entering a state of liminality. Jungian psychologists have studied liminality and how to move within this often-terrifying terrain. Jungian psychology views the gods of ancient Greece as archetypes within our psychological makeup. These gods constitute the archetypes on which our very culture is based. For example, Hippocrates, the father of medicine, was said to be a son of Asklepios, the god of healing. All physicians of today owe the existence of the physician and their craft to his archetypal influence. In ancient Greece, he had many healing centers, some concentrating on medicine and surgical practices, and others devoted to what could only be termed psychotherapy centers, where the priests of Asklepios cured patients by reading their dreams. Some other archetypes are: Zeus, the father archetype, Hera, the mother archetype, and Ares, the god of war. Many other exist, but we are interested in locating a god who can help us enter the state of liminality.

The Greek god Hermes is he who transgresses boundaries. He negotiates the boundary between consciousness and the unconscious and is the light-hearted bringer of sleep and dreams. As guide of souls in the Underworld (a place where all souls of the dead go and not to be confused with hell), Hermes also stands at the boundary between life and death, where life meets death and the two fuse. His mother, the goddess Maia, was associated with Heaven and Night. Everything around Hermes becomes ghostly. In the ancient Greek, Hermes is αγγελος, angel, messenger of the gods. He is also the protector of travelers. And in the sense that a novel is a journey into another world, Hermes is ever with the writer.

The creative act itself is a process of pulling material from both the personal and collective unconscious and depositing it in the author's consciousness. The fictional world has mythological characteristics and is close to the dream state ruled by Hermes. And, as one would expect, he is in constant companionship with the muses.[71] Hermes sits at this interface, along with the muses, dips his bucket into the cauldron of the unconscious, and dumps it into our consciousness, as shown in Figure 17.

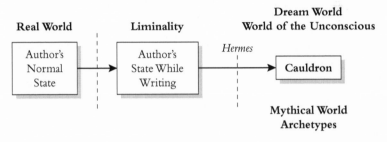

Figure 17

The primary characteristic of this mental state is a shift of the novelsmith's inner ground. His foundation is no longer firm, and he can be easily influenced, pushed and blown about by the winds of the unconscious. The author's sense of identity is suspended, and he becomes more susceptible to putting on another's persona and is able to speak with another's voice. While in liminality, the author is much more emotionally sensitive and open to input from both the personal and collective unconscious. He is up against the inner space inhabited by the "others," the anima/us.

The novelsmith then has three personifications of the entity that rules over the creative process: (1) the anima/us, (2) the muses, and (3) Hermes. Studying each of these further on your own may well provide you with further assistance in developing your creative process. In the next section, we'll further define what it feels like for the novelsmith to be in this state of liminality and receiving inspiration from the collective and personal unconscious.

THE WRITER AND THE CREATIVE PROCESS

At the beginning of this chapter, we talked about the information flowing into the novel as being from two sources: the world external to the author and that of his own internal world. The information flowing into the author from his internal world, while creating a novel, also involves processes that have a dual nature and can be segregated into two categories, as shown in Figure 18. The first is composed of those processes that spring from the author's intention, in that the author is in control of the incoming, consciously chosen, material; and the second is composed of those inspirational processes that force themselves upon him, rendering him somewhat helpless under their influence. Inspiration occurs mostly while in a state of liminality. While the author writes, he has little control over the material as it springs forth from his imagination because he has given up himself to his work.

Information Flow

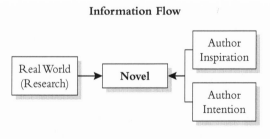

Figure 18

The Psychology of Creativity

All novels exist as works that come from both processes, no novel being solely the result of pure intention or inspiration. Jung says of the inspired work:

> These works positively force themselves on the author; his hand is seized, his pen writes things that his mind contemplates with amazement. ...the artist is not identical with the process of creation; he is aware that he is subordinate to his work or stands outside it, as though he were a second person; or as though a person other than himself had fallen within the magic circle of an alien will.[72]

This is the part of a novel that springs from the collective unconscious and is naturally archetypal. Jung describes the archetype as it occurs in literature:

> The primordial image, or archetype, is a figure—be it a daemon, a human being, or a process—that constantly recurs in the course of history and appears wherever creative fantasy is freely expressed. Essentially, therefore, it is a mythological figure. When we examine these images more closely, we find that they give form to countless typical experiences of our ancestors... In each of these images there is a little piece of human psychology and human fate, a remnant of the joys and sorrows that have been repeated countless times in our ancestral history, and on the average follow ever the same course. It is like a deeply graven river-bed in the psyche, in which the waters of life, instead of flowing along as before a broad but shallow stream, suddenly swell into a mighty river...

The Psychology of Creativity

> The moment when this mythological situation reappears is always characterized by a peculiar emotional intensity; it is as though chords in us were struck that had never resounded before, or as though forces whose existence we never suspected were unloosed... At such moments we are no longer individuals, but the race; the voice of all mankind resounds in us.[73]

The archetype will have this influence not only on the novel-smith while creating his novel while in the state of liminality, but also on the reader as he recreates the fictional world in his own mind. Remember that the reader has suspended disbelief, in a sense given up a part of himself, and passed over into a state that also resembles liminality and is also susceptible to the overwhelming influence of the archetype.

The influence of the archetype would then seem to be responsible for the unfathomable reception of books such as Richard Bach's *Jonathan Livingston Seagull* and Waller's *Bridges of Madison County*. In these works, word craft isn't so much the key to success as is the craft of honing the inspired material. What the author should keep in mind, however, is that the most powerful part of the novel will undoubtedly come from within the deep recesses of his own psyche while in a state of liminality.

★

You should now be able to understand the reasons that I wanted to lower your estimation of the information that flows into your novel from the outside world and to bolster your opinion of what comes from within you. Of the two worlds, the internal is even the more credible, because culture flows from the non-literal into the literal world. The internal is the most "real" because our perception of the external comes from, and maybe is even created by, the internal.

APPLICATION: How do I apply this to novelsmithing?

Okay then. This state of liminality is beginning to sound like the answer to the writer's dream of not only understanding the creative process but also of finding a way into it and controlling it. This is true to a surprising extent, and some methods of accessing it appear in many books on creative writing. "Free association" is a technique of scribbling down random thoughts, and it is used by many writers to unhook the imagination from the intellect and let it free-wheel. Of course, psychiatrists have used this since Freud invented psychotherapy. A few of these techniques are discussed in Janet Burroway's *Writing Fiction*.[74] They are good as far as they go, but let's investigate a couple of more direct methods of getting there.

The key, of course, is that liminality occurs close to the sleep state. So, we have two events where we are actually in a state of liminality: just before we go to sleep and just after we wake. Therefore, the best chance you have of being creative is to break out the notebook after you get into bed and again directly upon waking.

The first step is to scribble away until you get sleepy; however, you can carry this a step further. After you turn out the light, continue to concentrate on your story. If you have an inspiration, you can turn on the light, write it down, and turn off the light again. Don't consciously quit thinking about your novel. You probably won't get much out of this technique at first, but remember that developing this into a productive exercise is a process, and keep at it. This is where some of your most creative work will happen. Just as you're entering sleep, that state of liminality, if you can still focus on your novel, ideas will really start to blossom. On a personal note, I've spent as much as two hours turning the light on and off to get the inspiration down on paper and trying again to get to sleep. If you have a sleeping partner, this will drive them crazy, so it isn't for everyone.

The less trouble-prone option is to write directly upon waking. The trick here is to remember that the first thoughts you should allow into your mind must concern your novel. The human mind is a lot like a computer. The first thing you do with a computer in the morning is boot it. This loads the operating system into memory and allows it to function. During the waking process, we similarly activate the information we need to function during the day. We boot our brains. If, instead of showering, getting dressed, eating breakfast, and sorting out the day's activities, you immediately start thinking about your novel and planning the activities of your characters, you should find that writing will be relatively easy and ideas should flow freely.

I have performed both of these activities for several years, and found that thinking about my novel just before going to sleep primes me for even more creative work the next morning. At times when not bothered by outside distraction, I have worked continuously for as much as twenty-one hours. Once one of these marathon writing sessions is over, however, the following day or so can be rather uneventful on the writing front. I generally recover quickly.

The main point I want to make is this. Reaching and maintaining contact with Hermes' world of liminality is an art and an athletic feat all unto itself. The writer must experience that world, realize that it exists inside them, and learn to gain access to it. Going and coming easily takes practice. The writer has to train himself just as does a long distance runner. If you stop for a while, you lose your conditioning, and even if you gain access, your progress will be slow again at first. You won't have the stamina. It is a special state, and to gain access to it consistently requires special skills and continued practice.

A PERSONAL EXPERIENCE

At the risk of being accused of going off the beaten path, I'll relate the extremes to which I've gone to achieve the writing state. In December 1991, just before the Persian Gulf War, I decided to devote a month to a novel I'd been writing for the last few years. I had a rough draft, but the manuscript needed a concerted effort to make it into a full-fledged novel. I took the entire month off from my job and isolated myself at home. Since I was living alone at the time, this was relatively easy, and really not so unusual for a writer. But what I did next was a little unconventional.

I unplugged my TV and stereo, and covered all the clocks in my apartment. I vowed to leave my apartment only for food. I also vowed to think of nothing but the novel. When I went to bed at night, the last thing I thought about as sleep enveloped me was my novel. When I woke the next morning, the first thing I thought about, and the only thing I let myself think about, was my novel. I sat at my word processor from morning to night. I kept the curtains closed.

I allowed myself a single step outside in the morning to get the paper, since we were preparing for war in the Persian Gulf. Every morning I checked the headlines, then put it in the trash. No further word form the outside world was to creep into my isolation. I used my insomnia as an asset. When I woke, I wrote until I wanted to sleep. Then I slept. Daytime, nighttime, writing, sleep. It was all intertwined and unstructured. I didn't know if this would work. Could I write continuously for a month? Was it humanly possible? Would I go insane?

Yes, it worked. Yes, I wrote for a month, 24/7, without interruption. My single excursion to the supermarket was surreal. I found myself overly happy and emotionally volatile. Back home, it took no more than an hour to drop back into my writing mental state. My one contact with the external world was with the telephone. I did receive calls, but I initiated none on my own. I kept conversations short. Every time the phone rang, I nearly jumped out of my skin. Not only was the experiment a success, but it seemed to warp me in the right way. Since then, I've had no difficulty whatsoever with writer's block.

WRITER'S BLOCK

Now that we understand something about the creative state, we are also in a position to understand what goes wrong with it. Writer's block comes from losing contact with the liminal state of Hermes' world. Hermes has taken a hike, and to solve the problem, we need to find a way to coax him back.

Writer's block can be cured, and here I'll restate what I've said before. Since the writing "trance" is so close to the sleep state, the novelsmith suffering from writer's block should start thinking about his novel immediately upon waking, and even before getting out of bed. This loads the material in much the same way a computer boots. In that fresh state, the author's novel is put right up against the sleep state.

But the author can take that additional step in seeking a cure. Reviewing one's work late at night just before sleep also places it close to the dream state and better prepares one for immediate retrieval in the morning. If this all starts to sound as if you have to devote your entire existence to your writing, you're starting to get the right idea.

If you are blessed with insomnia, this gives you more time to write and at precisely the right time. I define insomnia as unusual awareness within the sleep state. You are still in Hermes' realm, so use him. These periods can be enormously creative. Don't fight insomnia. Use it.

DEPRESSION/PSYCHOSIS

In dealing with the deep reaches of our nature, we take certain risks. Generally, we encounter the unconscious during periods of crisis. This part of the psyche sleeps in its pale, complacent realm, but during crisis, it wakes, bringing with it all the elements of conflict. It then readies for the consciousness-raising, transcendent experience. That is the nature of the unconscious, and this is precisely the realm to which the author requests access. The result can be emotional instability. You can lose contact with reality. Frequently, the novelsmith is said by those around him to take on the neuroses of his characters. Family members complain about his irritability, moodiness.

Even worse, all this focus on the inner self can cause you to step into an unusual state of existence. In short, our lives can come to parallel those of myth, and when that happens, it wreaks havoc. We live out a Greek tragedy. As Murray Stein says in an essay titled *Hephaistos, A Pattern of Introversion*:

> Besides giving voice to the depth of experience and relating separate pieces of experience into a configuration, the connection of personal experience to myth can produce or

consolidate a psychological inflation (assimilation of the ego by the unconscious, often archetypal, content). The individual is unconsciously living a myth rather than a life. More accurately, an unconscious content is living him, rather than he it.[75]

A few years ago, a friend of mine, a non-writer, decided to become a mystery writer. After a few months of planning a novel, she abruptly quit. "My perception of people was changing," she said, "and not for the better." Everyone who writes should be aware of the dangers.

AUTHOR'S GLOW

In her book *The Writing Life*, Annie Dillard puts the author's feelings toward her own work in perspective:

> Another luxury for an idle imagination is the writer's own feeling about the work. There is neither a proportional relationship, nor an inverse one, between a writer's estimation of a work in progress and its actual quality. The feeling that the work is magnificent, and the feeling that it is abominable, are both mosquitoes to be repelled, ignored, or killed, but not indulged.

A little later in the same work she says again:

> This writing that you do, that so thrills you, that so rocks and exhilarates you, as if you were dancing next to the band, is barely audible to anyone else.

The Psychology of Creativity

Authors fall in love with their work. A friend of mine has termed this the "author's glow." The author's love for his own work can lead to a critical misjudging of it. Inspiration sweeps over us like an ocean wave, but all that gets to the page is little bits of life's debris like sifted sand. We have to learn to express inspiration in words that trigger a similar emotional experience in the reader. This is the novelsmith's burden.

EXERCISES
(a) Start a journal to log the time of the day you write, for how long, and your emotional state at the time, your degree of happiness. (b) Note in your journal any emotional states that correspond to those of your characters. (c) Note in your journal any unusual (for you) emotional states or ways of intellectualizing situations. (d) Note in your journal any deviations in your usual way of interacting with people. (e) Note in your journal where ideas seem to come from, paying particular attention to those that seem to come out of nowhere.

CHAPTER 11: The Ethics of Writing

Writing has long been thought to be of therapeutic value and, in many ways, cathartic. I have found this to be true myself, but I also believe that the processes involved are some of the most powerful in the human experience, and, therefore, may also be destructive when used naively or cruelly. The power of the written word has its source in the forces that create the universe. I believe it has the power to transform human existence. It behooves us all, as writers, to be careful how we use this power.

Since much of the novelsmith's inspiration comes from the collective unconscious and enters the story in the form of archetypes, it will be instructive to listen to what Carl Jung had to say about them and ethics:

> In itself, an archetype is neither good nor evil. It is morally neutral, like the gods of antiquity, and becomes good or evil only by contact with the conscious mind, or else a paradoxical mixture of both. Whether it will be conducive to good or evil is determined, knowingly or unknowingly, by the conscious attitude.
>
> In this way the work of the artist meets the psychic needs

of the society in which he lives, and therefore means more than his personal fate, whether he is aware of it or not. Being essentially the instrument of his work, he is subordinate to it, and we have no right to expect him to interpret it for us.[76]

With this statement by Jung in mind, when all is said and done, the author must evaluate his work for moral content and revise it accordingly, realizing that in its genesis, the work was amoral. After learning that a boy used one of his novels as a model to kill one of his fellow students and hold his class hostage, Stephen King expressed regret that he'd ever written the novel. We, as conscious, moral human beings, must realize that every human act contains within it the connotation of ethics. An author is responsible for what he dumps into the world.

Years ago, I backed off from a horror novel I had started. Something just seemed wrong about it, although I do not believe all horror is bad, and even believe Mary Shelley's *Frankenstein* to be one of the most important works of modern times. We should all keep an evaluative eye on the spirit we serve.

This really reflects back to the contract the author makes with the reader as a part of the Grand Illusion, as discussed in the chapter on narration. Remember that the reader has suspended disbelief. For the reader, this is a state of innocence and ethical vulnerability. The author has a moral responsibility toward his reader since the reader has voluntarily disarmed himself. Of course, the reader also has a responsibility to himself to question the ethical stance of any story, whether fiction or non-fiction.

In ancient times, the Greeks believed that ingenuity came from an even older religion, that of the Titans, and even more specifically from rebellious Prometheus. The Zeus religion, which

The Ethics of Writing

replaced that of the Titans, was based on wisdom, a higher form of consciousness. Wisdom carries with it the connotation of ethics, whereas ingenuity does not. Wisdom comes from a broader context that results from an ironic stance, a view of the subject matter from a higher perspective. The fact that irony carries with it a taste of the divine, as we discussed back in Chapter 5, indicates that this is where it starts to take on ethical connotations.

The author has already played his big cards in the beginning by the selection of Premise and narrative stance. At the end of the work, the novelsmith must assume a more adult role, and use what wisdom he can muster to control the ethical content of the work. Ultimately, Jung is correct: no one can tell what impact a work will have on the world, and the author must have a sort of faith that a higher order is involved.

EXERCISES
(a) Write a paragraph on the morality or immorality of your Premise. (b) Make a list of the possible ways your novel could be interpreted morally. (c) Write a paragraph on why you believe the world will be a better place with the publication of your novel.

CHAPTER 12: Writing, Rewriting, Editing

THE BAD FIRST DRAFT

They say Shakespeare never revised, nor did Mozart. However, the rest of us will have to slave over our work once it's "finished" to get it in shape to be published. Writing a novel is a bit like riding a wild horse bareback. You're astraddle all that energy, and you get thrown now and then. The horse never wants to stay on the trail, and much of the time you can't see it yourself. So you panic, knowing it's all slipping away. But writing a novel is also a little like preparing for a Broadway play. You'll have a lot of rehearsals, so maybe you'll get it right. The "rehearsals," of course, are the rewrites.

So now you have all your plotting, your chapter summaries, and all the research material you accumulated. Using all this material, you write each chapter. The first time through, the novelsmith works to find the story. In spite of all his preparation, he still struggles through the first draft, hoping that storyline he's following is a vein of gold. Here, he's working with caterpillars, backhoes, tractors. He moves earth around, creates gullies, hills, moves mountains. It's ugly, dirty work. He turns his chapter summaries into narration, setting, and scene.

Although the novelsmith tries for brilliance with all his might, the first time through is always a rough draft. You should allow yourself the freedom to write that bad first draft. Be fearless in your pursuit of storyline, using the central conflict as your guide, and let nothing slow your pace. The most important thing about it is not to be brilliant, but to get through it. You should write fast, and not look back. As Annie Dillard put it in *The Writing Life*:

> The reason not to perfect a work as it progresses is that... original work fashions a form the true shape of which it discovers only as it proceeds, so the early strokes are useless, however fine their sheen. Only when a paragraph's role in the context of the whole work is clear can the envisioning writer direct its complexity of detail to strengthen the work's ends.[77]

The more the novelsmith works the words, the more they become cast in concrete. You may not be able to change them later regardless of how badly they fit. You should leave it loose so that on the next pass you can work it in with the full context of the novel.

During this initial period of discovery, you do have your planning to guide you, but the energy in the story will constantly lead you astray. Pull it back in line as best you can and keep going. You may even be writing several chapters at once. While writing one, you'll realize how it affects another, and you'll be skipping back and forth scattering words like seeding a field of alfalfa. Keep from looking back as best you can. When you do, it'll be a horror show, but don't let that discourage you. The real writing is yet to come. If you keep going over it, polishing, you'll have difficulty swinging the ax later on. The less you like your work the first time through, the better off you are.

Writing, Rewriting, Editing

THE SECOND PASS

This is your first look at the full work, and your reaction is one of despair. What a pile of junk. Your older brother has been right all along. You really are a moron. But the novelsmith inside you knows that you should set the despair aside and get down to business. Now the novelsmith goes to work with the shovel, pick, hammer, chisel, the ax, maybe even a chain saw. During the rewrite, you will find the real story. You might even start to feel more confident about your Premise. You look again at structure, select which chapters fit, which should change place, which you have to cut. Use the Premise and novel geometry as a guide.

The novelsmith's attitude for the second pass: courage, ruthlessness, heartlessness. To really do some good, according to Eudora Welty, you have to "kill all your darlin's." In a similar vein, Samuel Johnson is supposed to have said, "Read over your composition and, when you meet a passage which you think is particularly fine, strike it out." Although I don't totally agree with this, I do believe you should realize that this is a process of getting rid of the fool's gold. The novelsmith's attempts at brilliance call attention to themselves and are generally disruptive. You can feel yourself trying to be a great writer instead of simply telling the story. Avoid the metaphysics. The "metaphysics" are the passages where you talk directly about the premise. Don't do it.

Examine each character, particularly minor ones, to make sure a change has occurred in each, that each has an "arc." Examine them to see if some might actually be the same character. If you have two characters that never appear together, or if one is present in the first half of the novel and the other in the second half, they may actually be the same character. This can come as a great surprise. These you can combine to great effect. You can also combine characters somewhat arbitrarily to make your characters more multi-dimensional. Another possibility, if you have a character that's not working, is to change the gender. This can really breathe life into not only the character but also the story.

The novel has to be written at least three times. The first time through yields raw material that has to be shaped into a more solidly constructed novel. It also insures you have found the premise and fully explored the subject. The second pass provides the novel with its proper shape. With the third pass, you get pickier.

THE THIRD PASS

Up until now, the novelsmith has been out in the field digging up his ore, and he has put it in the smelter to separate the metal from the slag. He has taken it out of the fire, placed it on his anvil and pounded it into the rough shape he's looking for. And now he goes to work with screwdrivers, pliers, tin snips, files, and wire-cutters. This is the tinkering stage, when he focuses on paragraphs, sentences, and words. It is also a purification process. As Leon Surmelion says:

> The writer purifies his ore to show the shining metal in it. He removes the insignificant, the irrelevant, and preserves only that which is essential to his purpose...[78]

Research has brought material from a lot of different sources, and you'll have to erase the seams, smooth over the narrative voice, and eliminate what you don't need. Everything must undergo the conversion so that it will fit into the fictional world. Remember that the craftsman is ever the enemy of the artist, in that you can tinker it to death, yet the art only shines through the use of craft.

Writing, Rewriting, Editing

PARAGRAPH STRUCTURE

Just like chapters, paragraphs give the reader breathing space. Most large paragraphs are actually multiple paragraphs and should be broken down. Don't think brilliance comes from writing long ones as did Russian novelists 150 years ago. On the other hand, don't use the carriage return as a substitute for inspiration, even though a short, one–sentence paragraph may add emphasis.

Craft your paragraphs with attention to reader needs and according to the topic at hand. You don't construct paragraphs as rigidly as you would in an essay (topic sentence, exposition, etc.), but you'll still find that frequently, they'll have the same characteristics. The writer of fiction is much more attuned to the flow of emotion, and emotional content will frequently determine a paragraph's structure and length.

SENTENCE STRUCTURE

Sentences are about thoughts. One that goes on too long can confuse the reader. On the other hand, long meandering sentences can be a part of the voice and give it an ethereal or even some other unimaginable quality. Consider Moly's monologue from *Ulysses* by James Joyce. It's the last chapter in the novel, and comes as one paragraph, thirty-six long pages without punctuations marks, apostrophes or any other niceties of the English language. It's written in what's known as "stream-of-consciousness," Here's a bit at the beginning:

> Yes because he never did a thing like that before as ask to get his breakfast in bed with a couple of eggs since the City Arms hotel when he used to be pretending to be laid up with

a sick voice doing his highness to make himself interesting for the old faggot Mrs Riordan that he thought he had a great leg of and she never left us a farthing all for masses for herself and her soul greatest miser ever was actually afraid to lay out 4d for her methyladted spirit telling me all her ailments...[79]

And here a little from the end of that chapter:

...and the sea the sea crimson sometimes like fire and the glorious sunsets and the figtrees in the Alameda gardens yes and all the queer little streets and the pink and blue and yellow houses and the rosegardens and the jessamine and geraniums and cactuses and Gibraltar as a girl where I was a Flower of the mountain yes when I put the rose in my hair like the Andalusian girls used or shall I wear a red yes and how he kidded me under the Moorish wall and I thought well as well him as another and then I asked him with my eyes to ask again yes and then he asked me would I yes to say yes my mountain flower and first I put my arms around him yes and drew him down to me so he could feel my breasts all perfume yes and his heart was going like mad and yes I said yes I will Yes.[80]

As you can see from these excerpts, let nothing stand in the way of what you're doing if you know your business and are good at it.

Avoid "false subject" sentences. They start out, "It is..." or "There is..." These are generic openings and will put your reader to sleep for the first two words. They are also statements of existence and will lead to a static narrative. Example: "There is a church on the hill overlooking the town and its people." Change this to: "The church on the hill overlooks the town and its people." Of course exceptions to this abound. Consider again the opening paragraph of Dickens' *A Tale of Two Cities*. "It was the best of times, it was the worst of times…"

Minimize passive voice sentence construction. Passive voice occurs when the subject of the sentence does not perform the action of the verb. The actor is left out of the sentence completely in passive voice. Example: "The book was put on the shelf." Note that we don't know who performed the action; therefore, the action has lost the human element. Correction: "James put the book on the shelf." Now we have a character in the story, and the difference is crucial to good storytelling.

WORDS

Keep it simple. Use "use" instead of "utilize," "to" stead of "in order to" (has nothing to do with ordering), no "suddenly's," and don't use "very" very often. Remember that the most profound statement in all English literature consists of only six words, two of them repeats, all of one syllable, only one of them more than two letters: "To be or not to be?" Words gather importance through context. Don't be pedantic by throwing big words around. Don't be verbose. View every word with suspicion. Remember that the reader isn't interested in you, he is interested in the story. If you want to be really smart, just tell the story.

Use the skills of the poets. Most of us are aware of rhyme, but it should be minimized in narrative fiction. On the other hand, some of the more obscure techniques are the prose writer's bread and butter:

Assonance: Repetition of vowels without repetition of consonants (as in stony and holy).

Alliteration: Repetition of initial consonant sounds in two or more neighboring words (as in the terrible twos).

Rhythm: An ordered recurrent alternation of strong and weak elements in the flow of sound and silence in speech. Consider the opening to Hemingway's *For Whom the Bell Tolls*:

> He lay flat on the brown, pine-needled floor of the forest, his chin on his folded arms, and high overhead the wind blew in the tops of the pine trees.[81]

The natural "beat" of the individual words, accompanied by assonance and alliteration, create the rhythm in this sentence and take it to the level of prose poetry.

But don't make your work overly poetic. These techniques should be used when the mood and tone are right for it. Use them in situations of heightened tension, when the commonness of reality metamorphoses into the surreal landscape of escalating human emotion.

Editing is itself a skill and must be continually developed. A highly skilled novelsmith can slave over his work for months to good effect, while a less skilful one will perhaps even do it damage. Work on your writing skills every day of your life. You never become so proficient that you can't improve. The way you use words is your bread and butter. Don't become arrogant about it. Your writing should grow every day until you die.

While writing the novel over and over, the author builds on the material and provides clarity and precision. He also finds the hidden significance of events and uncovers unintended relationships. This "worrying" until the story fully exposes itself is a necessary part of the craft. Some elements will be hypergolic, igniting on contact. Other elements will be synergistic, will become more than the sum of the parts.

Though you probably don't want to hear it, you'll have to edit your novel again sometime in the future. You should let it set a while to gain distance, perspective. Some authors say, jokingly, that they paste it on the wall, back up and read it through binoculars. You can gain distance from a work by letting it set for a day, weeks, months, years. The point is, a gestation period is required to gain distance so that the imperfections become visible to the novelsmith.

THE SENSES

During all the rewriting, find ways to integrate the senses into the narrative, all five senses. The senses are so difficult to deal with that you should never be complacent about them, and during the edit phase, you'll have the time to ensure you haven't left them out where they are needed. Always keep them in the back of your mind. I'll say it again: The reader suffers from total sensory deprivation in the fictional world. Without the character's feelings, he has no contact with that world.

GETTING IT CRITIQUED

Unless you're in a writing group, the first to see your work will be family and friends. This may lead to all sorts of strange responses. First of all, be assured that if you've written it in first person (POV), they'll believe that you're the character doing the talking and that the story is about your family. After reading the first chapter of my novel set in my hometown, my mother called me and bawled me out, saying that none of that happened, as if it was about our family. I've talked to many other writers who've had similar experiences. In spite of this, I do have a sister-in-law who always sees my work first, and before it's complete. Generally, I say don't give it to anyone close to you, particularly a family member. You don't need the grief.

WRITING GROUPS

I continue to be amazed at the subtlety and complexity of a novel. A friend of mine in Colorado has a degree in creative writing and whines that it doesn't help him at all. The founder of the Rocky Mountain Writers Guild in Boulder is fond of saying that the reason he's never been able to get a novel published is that he is too educated. He has a PhD in literature.

To bolster my writing skills and confidence, I've engaged in a wide array of activities. I started out by taking creative and critical writing at the University of Colorado, and classes in the American novel. I attended both the Aspen Writers Conference and the Sierra Writing Camp. While living in Boulder, Colorado, I was a member of the Rocky Mountain Writers Guild for seven years. I served on its Board of Directors, attended its novel workshops and was a member of its Live Poets Society. I was the founding member of the Guild's Literary Society and chaired its meetings. I supervised the publication of and provided articles for the Guild's newsletter. I also founded an independent writing group that consisted of six members and lasted for eight years. All this helped me to feel like a writer, and I'd advise you to become a member of some group that will help you think of yourself as one.

But writing groups can also be problematic. When you walk into a bookstore, in all probability, 99% of everything on the shelf won't interest you. Don't think that when you walk into a critique group that all those there will be in tune with what you've written. You'll get a wide variety of opinions about it. You should look for that one special reader, one who is supportive, under-stands your work as you do, and can provide valuable insight into its shortcomings.

Realize the limitations of writing groups. Rarely can any-one in a writing group help you with the overall novel because they see it in bits and pieces. Besides, rarely does anyone know anything about the overall structure of a novel. The good critics provide support and creative criticism. The bad ones stifle origi-nality and critique toward the stereotypical. The ugly ones harbor jealousy and unleash harsh criticism.

The first law of getting your work critiqued is: It's your job to protect your work from criticism. The second law is: Criticism cures delusion. By not accepting criticism, you tend to live with a false reality about how good your writing is. My advice is to put your work out there to good critics for a while, perhaps even a couple of years, but eventually, you should quit. Writing tends to correct itself if you do it long enough because your craft matures.

WORKING WITH AN EDITOR

Many writers work with a professional editor, and they pay them for their expertise. By a professional editor, I mean one with a B.A. in English at least and preferably an M.A. You can have them both story edit and copy edit. You don't run onto these people at the corner drugstore, but look around on the Internet. You just might find someone who can really help you. Always have your manuscript professional edited before you send it to an agent or publisher.

CRITIQUING

Everyone who engages in this activity should remember

that critiquing is, by its very nature, illicit. It's a violation of the author/reader contract. The reader and the author have an agreement. The first law of imaginative literature is that the author writes fiction as if it is the truth, and the reader *suspends disbelief*. That *is* the contract. So any reader who critiques violates that contract since he casts a suspicious eye upon it under the pretext of judging its merits. If you talk to a psychologist, he'll tell you that, along with the critic's best intentions, he always comes to the process with a touch of anger, just a smidgen of irritation at the edge of the mind. That's the nature of critiquing. The critic should keep this in mind while reading the work.

What can we do, as critics of our peers' work, to redeem the situation? Several laws apply. The first law of critiquing is the same as it is for doctors: First and foremost, do no harm. This is a great deal more difficult than you might think. The inclination is to critique toward the stereotypical and stifle creativity to protect conventional standards for writing. The standard rules, however, all go out the window for fiction. The work establishes its own standards, and the role of the critic is then to judge the effectiveness of the writing, whether it impacts the reader. Each of us will have different opinions on that, since we all have different tastes in fiction. Critiquing is subjective. Samuel R. Delany's science fiction novel *Dhalgren* starts this way:

> to wound the autumnal city.
> So howled out for the world to give him a name.
> The in-dark answered with wind.
> All you know I know: careening astronauts and bank clerks glancing at the clock before lunch; actresses cowling at light-ringed mirrors and freight elevator operators grinding a

thumbful of grease on a steel handle…[83]

What would you do with this in a critique group? Go on, admit it. You'd trash it. Yet, it passed the scrutiny of world-class editors.

The second law of critiquing is: Praise the art and critique the craft. But can art and craft be separated? Here are some definitions I find useful:

> Art: (1) the conscious use of skill and creative imagination,[84] (2) the application of skill, knowledge, etc., in a creative effort to produce works that have form or beauty, esthetic expression of feeling, etc.[85]
>
> Craft: (1) skill in planning, making or executing,[86] (2) skill or ingenuity in any calling, especially in a manual employment.[87]

As you can see, art and craft tend to merge in these definitions. I would prefer to define them as follows:

> Art: That uncontrollable element of the work that comes from inspiration.
>
> Craft: That element of the work under the control of the author.

Although they do tend to separate in these definitions, the two are still Siamese twins, inseparable but somehow distinguishable. Learn to recognize the difference and critique with a planned, compassionate strategy instead of "shooting from the hip." Being supportive of the artistic elements will encourage the writer, and he will always appreciate knowing the imperfections in his craft.

Don't critique toward what you like, but toward strengthening

the elements already in the work. Hemingway would be shred-
ded in a writing group. His prose is too stark and sparse. Faulkner
would be laughed out of the room. His opening to *The Sound and
the Fury* is practically unreadable unless you know the narrator is
unreliable: a thirty-three year old mentally retarded man. If we
could have gotten our hands on that before it was published, we
could have "straightened it out."

The third law of critiquing is: It's not your job to save the author from himself. Unburden yourself as a critic. Realize that the
author is responsible for his own work, and that if you don't get
your say, if you occasionally or even repeatedly pull your punches,
the world may be a better place for it.

The German poet Rainer Maria Rilke once wrote to a young
admirer:

> Works of art are of an infinite loneliness and with nothing so
> little to be reached as with criticism. Only love can grasp and
> hold and be just toward them.[88]

EXERCISES
(a) Make a list of the ways you plan to get your novel critiqued
while in the process of writing it. (b) Develop a plan for getting
the complete ms critiqued before making the final edits. (c) Make
a list of your skills that qualify you to critique someone else's
work. (d) Write a paragraph on your particular critiquing method.

CHAPTER 13: Publishing

THE FINISHED MANUSCRIPT

The completed manuscript (ms) has a specific format. On the first page, at the top left, put your name and address. Also, include your telephone number and email address. On the upper right, put the number of words in your manuscript. This constitutes the heading of the first page. Right after this (still on the first page), center the following: the novel's title in capital letters, followed two lines later by CHAPTER 1, and two lines after that, the first paragraph of the novel. The text of the manuscript follows this same format. Each chapter starts on a new page. At the very end of the manuscript you put the words THE END, centered two lines after the last word of the novel.

The body of the manuscript should be double-spaced, left-justified, and with the right edge uneven. Agents and publishers consider it unprofessional to justify the text. Margins should be at least one inch on all sides and not exceed 1.25 inches. The author's last name, the title, or a shortened version of it, and the page number should appear at the upper right of each page, except for the first page.

The font should be 12 point and have a "clean" appearance on the full page. Some fonts, although they appear fine as individual letters, bleed into each other and generally give off strange visual effects when you see a full page. You should have 250-300 words per page, but this will be determined by your font and margins. A published novel can have almost any number of words, depending on the format the publisher chooses. *The Bridges of Madison County* has approximately 250 words per page, *Red Storm Rising* about 500. The manuscript should be no more than 100,000 words. Unpublished authors have a particularly difficult time getting a long novel published, but you will see it happen occasionally. Be forewarned that the longer the first novel, the more difficult it will be to get published.

THE DON'TS

- Don't use a separate cover sheet or title page.
- No fancy fonts.
- No script texts (*like this*).
- No large fancy first-letters of the first words of chapters, as they sometimes appear in a published novel. The manuscript is a bland, no frills presentation of the text.
- Don't try to imitate the format of a published novel. This is a manuscript, not a book.
- Don't put it in a binder. Manuscripts are loose-leaf.
- Don't use a cover illustration.

RESEARCHING THE MARKET

Once the manuscript is complete, it's time to try to get a literary agent. Hopefully, all during the time you're writing your novel you are also researching the marketplace to see what's out there that resembles your novel. If you write genre fiction, your task will be easier. If you've written something a little more original, you'll have a task ahead of you.

While you write, read and search for highly acclaimed novels with which to compare yours. Each novel should have an "acknowledgements" section, in which the author may mention his agent or editor. This type of information will give you a first guess at who might want to represent or publish your novel.

FINDING AN AGENT

In Chapter 1, you determined what type of novel you were planning to write. Now you can put that information to good use. Agents are specialized. Your job is to match your work with an agent who sells that type of novel.

The first step is to find agents who belong to the Association of Authors Representatives (AAR). I recommend dealing only with AAR members; otherwise, you open yourself up to all sorts of scams and unethical agents, many of whom will want to edit your manuscript for a small fortune. Don't fall for it. Real agents aren't editors. AAR can be reached on the web at aaronline.org. You'll find the names and addresses of almost all AAR agents at the website, and even more importantly, the agency web address. Find a specific agent who might be interested in representing your work.

Good agents are being bombarded with hundreds, if not thousands, of proposals every year. So you're up against a difficult task. Do your homework. The more you know about the agent you're querying, the better chance you have at making a favorable impression. Landing a New York City agent is preferable because that's where most of the publishing houses are located, but once you've exhausted them, you'll find good agents spread across the United States, particularly on the West Coast.

Publishing

THE QUERY LETTER

Limit yourself to three, at most four, paragraphs, hopefully on a single page. State in the opening of your letter what you have and why you believe they may be interested in representing it. Your one-sentence summary of your novel will also go into the first paragraph. The one-paragraph statement of the storyline will constitute the second paragraph, with perhaps a few modifications. The third paragraph will be about yourself, and hopefully convince the agent that you are sane, educated, know your subject and have good writing skills. That's it. Offer to provide the full manuscript, and close with "Sincerely," etc.

Lastly, if you can't determine whether the agency represents your type of novel, call the agency, but only to ensure that the agency still exists and to get a contact name for the query. Don't try a sales pitch.

WHAT TO SEND

1. Query letter to a specific person at the agency.
2. First ten pages or so, maybe as many as fifty, depending on agency guidelines, if you can determine them.
3. Synopsis, up to twenty pages, if the agency guidelines so state. Many agencies don't want a detailed synopsis. The synopsis is your collection of chapter summaries.
4. Include return postage and packaging. Include a SASE (self-addressed, stamped envelope). If you forget the SASE, you will most certainly be rejected out of hand and never hear a word.

You should use a paper clip to hold all pages together, but don't staple any of it.

Publishing

Query approximately 100 agents, all simultaneously. A few will receive your elaborate package, but most should get only your query letter and first chapter (~ten pages). The postage alone will probably put you in the poor house.

AGENT RESPONSES

Responses come in many forms. Some (most) will be form-letters addressed to "Dear Author." Occasionally, you'll get a personal response. Don't let any of them discourage you. Persistence in the face of rejection is the name of the game.

SENDING OUT THE FULL MANUSCRIPT

Hopefully, your query letter will generate some interest. Depending on the type of novel you've written and how well you've targeted your marketing, you may have as many as fifty percent of the agents request the full manuscript. But more likely you'll get about ten percent or less who are interested.

Most agents will request the manuscript on an exclusive basis. This means that you can't send the full manuscript to anyone else while they have it. I have mixed feelings about complying with this, because agents won't generally do what they say they'll do anyway. Some will respond immediately, but others will wait months. I would at least consider sending it out to several agents (if you are so lucky to have that many interested) simultaneously, even if they request it exclusively. Just don't tell them what you're doing. The chance that any one of them will accept the novel is still slim, and if one says he'll take it, you can always tell the others you want your manuscript back without giving a reason. You should be so lucky as to have two agents who want it simultaneously.

Publishing

CAUTIONS:
1. Don't pay a reading fee to an agency. AAR specifically forbids their agents to do this.
2. Avoid any agency that wants to edit your novel for a price. This is a scam. Some charge as much as $125 per hour. No reputable agency, particularly not one that belongs to AAR, will do this. Reputable agents will either accept or reject your manuscript.

Some agents will respond immediately, usually those most interested, and some will take several months. A few agents will never respond at all. Once eighty percent of the responses have come in, and your complete ms has been rejected several times, you'll know whether you want to either pursue getting an agent or decide you've had enough crap from them and try to get a publisher instead.

LOOKING FOR A PUBLISHER

Most large publishing houses will no longer consider a submission from an unagented author. However, most midrange and small publishing houses will accept manuscripts directly and from unagented authors. Soho Press is one. Search the Internet for publisher websites, and follow their instructions. Their submission requirements will generally be much like those for agents. You can use the query letter and synopsis you used to look for an agent, with a few obvious modifications. This time you'll be looking for what's called an "acquisitions editor." The same rules apply. Acquisitions editors deal with specific types of books, so try to find all the information you can on each person. Find out what type of books they purchase, and what they expect in a query. If you can't find out any other way, call the publishing house. Again, don't try to sell your novel. Be business-like, get the information you're after and hang up.

DON'T GIVE UP!!!

I've had several friends who wrote great novels, received rejections from ten or so agents, tried ten or so publishers, got more rejections and quit. On the other hand, Stephen White (a psychologist who lives in Boulder, Colorado and writes psychological thrillers) wrote his first novel (*Privileged Information*) and tried for two years to get an agent/publisher and failed totally. Then, he talked to a friend who had a contact at Viking and the magic happened. The book became a best seller, so much so that Stephen had to quit his practice as a psychotherapist so he could devote all his time to writing.

LIFE AFTER PUBLICATION

A good friend of mine, who recently published her first novel, had a dream experience (but a real one) after a publishing house accepted her novel. She flew to New York, met her agent and publisher, went out to dinner with them (at the agent's expense), and generally had a marvelous time. Her editor did an excellent job editing the novel with no disagreements, and generally improved the work.

But after the book was published, the publisher slumped into the background, didn't promote it at all, and it didn't sell well. It did receive favorable reviews, even in the *New York Times Book Review*.

Publishers generally put their marketing dollars into books that sell well after the first couple of weeks. Don't expect your publisher to do all the publicity. You may have to hit the trail on your own, at your own expense, and even have to contact bookstores to set up signings.

SELF-PUBLISHING

Self-publishing may not be your last choice but your first. If you have a small target market, and don't want to run the agent/publisher gauntlet, you can publish it yourself rather easily through a print on demand (POD) service. Some of the more common ones are iUniverse, Publish America, and CreateSpace. Both iUniverse and Publish America will edit your work (for a fee) and print the book in either cloth or paperback. Checkout their different packages at their websites.

CreateSpace, a member of the Amazon.com group of companies, will publish your novel in paperback for no charge. You only pay for proof copies and any other final copies you want for your own use. You have to supply them with PDF files of your cover and internal text, formatted to their specifications. You can either supply the ISBN or they will supply one at no charge. If you supply the ISBN, then you are the listed publisher. If CreateSpace supplies the ISBN, they will be listed as the publisher. Your book will also appear in Books In Print and Barnes & Noble. Check the CreateSpace website for further details. Check the R. R. Bowker website to find out how to purchase an ISBN. Anyone can buy one. CreateSpace books are listed on Amazon and are listed as "in stock" and are immediately available. If you sign up for an Amazon Seller Central Account, your book will appear with the "Look Inside" feature, which allows the customer to view several pages and also search the book's text.

Publishing it for mobile devices is another option that has

unlimited potential for the future. Amazon's Kindle, which uses an electronic-paper that displays letters in E Ink, has attracted a lot of attention. Sony also has a Reader Digital Book that is quite popular. Putting your book on Apple's iPhone, iPod Touch, or iPad is also possible, but requires some programming knowledge to develop an application, which then must be approved by Apple.

The publishing world is changing rapidly. No telling what the publishing landscape will look like by the time you finish your novel. Stay abreast of the industry by periodically checking Publishers Weekly and comparable Web sites.

EXERCISES

(a) State your goals for getting your novel published. (b) Identify the target market for your novel. (c) Make a list of agents who might be interested in representing your work. (d) Make a list of publishers who might want to publish your work. (e) Write a query letter.

CHAPTER 14: Final Thoughts

Writing a novel will probably be the most complex and intellectually challenging project you'll ever undertake. Proper preparation and attention to craft is crucial to seeing the project through to a successful conclusion. That has been the sole purpose of this narrative. Academics have struggled for generations trying to teach the subject, and to my way of thinking, not done very well because they teach novel writing as a part of creative writing rather than as a separate, more advanced, subject. You have to include the entire subject if you want to teach the basics of novelsmithing.

I would just like to repeat my words of caution. What you have learned from these pages should not be taken as dogma. Locking into a process like this can stifle your creativity. Many great novels would be difficult to analyze in these terms. What this approach should provide is a structure through which you can unlock many of the forces at work in literature. But trust to the dictates of the story you are telling.

You might stop by www.novelsmithing.com, and its associated blog, from time to time to see what's up. I plan to maintain the website into the foreseeable future.

Good luck.

Attachments

ATTACHMENT I – Genesis of the Big Idea.

From Henry James, "Preface to *The Spoils of Poynton.*"

It was years ago, I remember, one Christmas Eve when I was dining with friends: a lady beside me made in the course of talk one of those allusions that I have always found myself recognising on the spot as "germs." The germ, wherever gathered, has ever been for me the germ of a "story," and most of the stories straining to shape under my hand have sprung from a single small seed, a seed as minute and wind-blown as that casual hint for "The Spoils of Poynton" dropped unwittingly by my neighbour, a mere floating particle in the stream of talk. What above all comes back to me with this reminiscence is the sense of the inveterate minuteness, on such happy occasions, of the precious particle—reduced, that is, to its mere fruitful essence. ….

So it was, at any rate, that when my amiable friend, on the Christmas Eve, before the table that glowed safe and fair through the brown London night, spoke of such an odd matter as that a good lady in the north, always well looked on, was at daggers drawn with her only son, ever hitherto exemplary, over the ownership of the valuable furniture of a fine old house just accruing to the young man by his father's death, I instantly became aware, with my "sense for the subject," of the prick of inoculation; the *whole* of the virus, as I have called it, being infused by that single touch. There had been but ten words, yet I had recognised in them, as in a flash, all the possibilities of the little drama of my "Spoils," which glimmered then and there into life.

Attachments

ATTACHMENT II – Discovering Story Structure.

From Henry James, "Preface to *The American.*"

It had come to me, this happy, halting view of an interesting case, abruptly enough, some years before: I recall sharply the felicity of the first glimpse, though I forget the accident of thought that produced it. I recall that I was seated in an American "horse-car" when I found myself, of a sudden, considering with enthusiasm, as the theme of the "story," the situation, in another country and an aristocratic society, of some robust but insidiously beguiled and betrayed, some cruelly wronged [1], compatriot: the point being in especial that he should suffer at the hands of persons pretending to represent the highest possible civilization and to be of an order in every way superior to his own [2]. What would he "do" in that predicament, how would he right himself, or how, failing a remedy, would he conduct himself under his wrong? This would be the question involved, and I remember well how, having entered the horse-car without a dream of it, I was presently to leave that vehicle in full possession of my answer. He would behave in the most interesting manner—it would all depend on that: stricken, smarting, sore, he would arrive at his just vindication and then would fail of all triumphantly and all vulgarly enjoying it [3]. He would hold his revenge and cherish it and feel its sweetness, and then in the very act of forcing it home would sacrifice it in disgust. He would let them go [4], in short, his haughty contemners, even while feeling them, with joy, in his power, and he would obey, in so doing, one of the large and easy impulses *generally* characteristic of his type. He wouldn't "forgive"—that would have, in the case, no application; he would simply turn, at the

Attachments

supreme moment, away, the bitterness of his personal loss yielding to the very force of his aversion [5]. All he would have at the end would be therefore just the moral convenience, indeed the moral necessity, of his practical, but quite unappreciated, magnanimity [6]; and one's last view of him would be that of a strong man indifferent to his strength and too wrapped in fine, too wrapped above all in *other* and intenser, reflections for the assertion of his "rights." This last point was of the essence and constituted in fact the subject: there would be no subject at all, obviously,—or simply the commonest of the common,—if my gentleman should enjoy his advantage.

[1] First Plot Point
[2] Beginning, the conflict locked
[3] Mid Novel Reversal
[4] Second Plot Point
[5] Ending
[6] Premise: Magnanimity overcomes cruelty.

Attachments

ATTACHMENT III – Chapter Structure

From *Moby Dick*, by Herman Melville

CHAPTER 47. The Mat-Maker

It was a cloudy, sultry afternoon; the seamen were lazily loung-
ing about the decks, or vacantly gazing over into the lead-colored
waters. Queequeg and I were mildly employed weaving what is
called a sword-mat, for an additional lashing to our boat. So still
and subdued and yet somehow preluding was all the scene, and
such an incantation of revelry lurked in the air, that each silent
sailor seemed resolved into his own invisible self. [a]

I was the attendant or page of Queequeg, while busy at the
mat. As I kept passing and repassing the filling or woof of marline
between the long yarns of the warp, using my own hand for the
shuttle, and as Queequeg, standing sideways, ever and anon slid his
heavy oaken sword between the threads, and idly looking off upon
the water, carelessly and unthinkingly drove home every yarn; I
say so strange a dreaminess did there then reign all over the ship
and all over the sea, only broken by the intermitting dull sound
of the sword, that it seemed as if this were the Loom of Time,
and I myself were a shuttle mechanically weaving and weaving
away at the Fates. There lay the fixed threads of the warp subject
to but one single, ever returning, unchanging vibration, and that
vibration merely enough to admit of the crosswise interblending
of other threads with its own. This warp seemed necessity; and
here, thought I, with my own hand I ply my own shuttle and
weave my own destiny into these unalterable threads. Meantime,

Attachments

Queequeg's impulsive, indifferent sword, sometimes hitting the woof slantingly, or crookedly, or strongly, or weakly, as the case might be; and by this difference in the concluding blow producing a corresponding contrast in the final aspect of the completed fabric; this savage's sword, thought I, which thus finally shapes and fashions both warp and woof; this easy, indifferent sword must be chance—aye, chance, free will, and necessity—no wise incompatible—all interweavingly working together. The straight warp of necessity, not to be swerved from its ultimate course—its every alternating vibration, indeed, only tending to that; free will still free to ply her shuttle between given threads; and chance, though restrained in its play within the right lines of necessity, and sideways in its motions directed by free will, though thus prescribed to by both, chance by turns rules either, and has the last featuring blow at events. [b]

★

Thus we were weaving and weaving away when I started at a sound so strange, long drawn, and musically wild and unearthly, that the ball of free will dropped from my hand, and I stood gazing up at the clouds when that voice dropped like a wing. High aloft in the cross-trees was that mad Gay-Header, Tashtego. His body was reaching eagerly forward, his hand stretched out like a wand, and at brief sudden intervals he continued his cries. To be sure the same sound was that very moment perhaps being heard all over the seas, from hundreds of whalemen's look-outs perched as high in the air; but from few of those lungs could that accustomed old cry have derived such a marvellous cadence as from Tashtego the Indian's.

As he stood hovering over you half suspended in air, so wildly and eagerly peering towards the horizon, you would have thought him some prophet or seer beholding the shadows of Fate, and by those wild cries announcing their coming. [c]

"There she blows! there! there! there! she blows! she blows!"

"Where-away?"

"On the lee-beam, about two miles off! a school of them!"

Instantly all was commotion.

The Sperm Whale blows as a clock ticks, with the same undeviating and reliable uniformity. And thereby whale-men distinguish this fish from other tribes of his genus.

"There go flukes!" was now the cry from Tashtego; and the whales disappeared.

"Quick, steward!" cried Ahab. "Time! time!"

Dough-Boy hurried below, glanced at the watch, and reported the exact minute to Ahab.

The ship was now kept away from the wind, and she went gently rolling before it. Tashtego reporting that the whales had gone down heading to leeward, we confidently looked to see them again directly in advance of our bows. For that singular craft at times evinced by the Sperm Whale when, sounding with his head in one direction, he nevertheless, while concealed beneath the surface, mills around, and swiftly swims off in the opposite quarter—this deceitfulness of his could not now be in action; for there was no reason to suppose that the fish seen by Tashtego had been in any way alarmed, or indeed knew at all of our vicinity. One of the men selected for shipkeepers—that is, those not appointed to the boats, by this time relieved the Indian at the mainmast head. The sailors at the fore and mizzen had come down; the line tubs were fixed in their places; the cranes were thrust out; the mainyard was backed, and the three boats swung over the sea like three samphire baskets over high cliffs. Outside of the bulwarks their eager crews with one hand clung to the rail, while one foot was expectantly poised on the gunwale. So look the long line of man-of-war's men about to throw themselves on board an enemy's ship. [d]

But at this critical instant a sudden exclamation was heard that took every eye from the whale. With a start all glared at dark Ahab, who was surrounded by five dusky phantoms that seemed fresh formed out of air. [e]

Things to note:

[a]   Establishing the setting.

[b]   Introducing the primary processes.

[c]   Defining the event that advanced the storyline.

[d]   Defining the action.

[e]   Identifying the mystery for the next chapter.

Processes described: weaving, whaling, sailing, mythology.

Endnotes

[1] Forbes, R. J., *Studies in Ancient Technology*, Vol. VIII, Leiden: E. J. Brill, 1971, page 78.

[2] Furley, William D., *Studies in the Use of Fire in Ancient Greek Religion*, Salem: Ayer Company, Publishers, Inc., 1988, page i.

[3] Homer, *The Iliad*, tr. by Martin Hammond, New York: Penguin Books, 1987, page 321.

[4] As a fine example, see, von Bothmer, Dietrich, *The Amasis Painter and His World, Vase-Painting in Sixth-Century B.C. Athens*, New York: Thames and Hudson ltd., and Malibu: The J. Paul Getty Museum, 1985, page 44-55.

[5] Burroway, Janet, *Writing Fiction, A Guide to Narrative Craft*, New York: Longman, 2000, page 312.

[6] Kundera, Milan, *The Art of the Novel*, New York: Harper & Row, Publishers, Inc., 1988, page 35.

[7] James, Henry, *The Art of the Novel*, New York: Charles Schribner's Sons, 1934 (1907), page 48.

[8] Wellek, René, and Austin Warren, *Theory of Literature*, New York: Harcourt, Brace & World, Inc., 1956, page 206.

[9] Aristotle, *The Complete Works of Aristotle*, Princeton: Princeton University Press, 1984, page 2322.

[10] For a somewhat different take on Premise, see *The Art of Dramatic Writing, Its Basis in the Creative Interpretation of Human Motives*, Chapter I, by Lajos Egri, New York: Simon & Schuster, Inc., 1960.

[11] James, Henry, *The Art of the Novel*, New York: Charles Schribner's Sons, 1934, page 15.

[12] For a somewhat different approach to story structure, see *Screenplay, The Foundations of Screenwriting*, by Syd Field, New York: Dell Publishing, 1984.

[13] For further information, see *The Elements of Screenwriting, A Guide for Film*

Endnotes

and Television Writing, By Irwin R. Blacker, New York: Collier Books, 1986.

[14] Fitzgerald, F. Scott, *The Great Gatsby,* New York: Charles Scribner's Sons, 1925, page 121.

[15] Colebrook, Claire, *Irony,* New York: Routledge, 2004, page 27.

[16] Moore, T. Sturge, *Art and Life,* London: Methuen, 1910, page 232.

[17] Mantel, Hilary, *Beyond Black,* New York: Henry Holt and Company LLC, 2004, pages 3-4.

[18] Homer, *The Iliad,* tr. by Robert Fitzgerald, Franklin Center: The Franklin Library, 1952, page 47.

[19] Euripides, *Euripides: Bacchae, Iphigenia at Aulis, Rhesus,* ed. and tr. by David Kovacs, Cambridge: Harvard University Press, LCL, 2002, page 201.

[20] Eliot, George, *Adam Bede,* New York: Charles Schribner's Sons, 1917, page 1.

[21] Melville, Herman, *Moby Dick or, the Whale,* New York: Dell Publishing Co., Inc., 1959, page 27.

[22] However, Dostoevsky did not burn everything and start from scratch, as he said and many have reported. For a detailed account of his search for a narrative scheme, see Frank, Joseph, *Doestoevsky, The Miraculous Years, 1865-1871,* Princeton: Princeton University Press, 1995, Chapter 6, especially page 93.

[23] McInerney, Jay, *Bright Lights, Big City.* New York: Vintage Books, 1984, page 1.

[24] Whiteley, Opal, *The Singing Creek Where the Willows Grow, The Rediscovered Diary of Opal Whiteley,* presented by Benjamin Hoff, New York: Ticknor & fields, 1986, page 81.

[25] Homer, *The Odyssey,* tr. by Robert Fitzgerald, Franklin Center: The Franklin Library, 1978, page 3.

[26] Hansen, Ron, *Mariette in Ecstasy,* New York: Edward Burlingame Books, 1991, page 29.

[27] Pirsig, Robert, *Zen and the Art of Motorcycle Maintenance, An Inquiry into Values.* New York: Bantam Books, 1974, page 3.

Endnotes

[28] Dickens, Charles, *A Tale of Two Cities*, New York: Vintage Books, 1990, page 7.

[29] Walker, Alice, *The Color Purple*, New York: Pocket Books, 1982, page 1.

[30] Liddell & Scott, *An Intermediate Greek-English Lexicon*, pg 230.

[31] Hesiod, *Works and Days*, lines 45-60.

[32] Kerenyi, C., *The Gods of the Greeks*, New York: Thames and Hudson, 1951, page 207.

[33] Colebrook, Claire, *Irony*, London: Routledge, 2004, page 135.

[34] Ibid, page 23.

[35] Ibid, page 20.

[36] Ibid, page 27.

[37] Ibid, page 180.

[38] Hemingway, Ernest, *For Whom the Bell Tolls*, New York: Charles Scribner's Sons, 1940, page 173.

[39] Ibid, page 22.

[40] Bradbury, Ray, *The Martian Chronicles*, New York: Bantam Books, 1958, page 80.

[41] de Santillana, Giorgio, *The Origins of Scientific Thought, From Anaximander to Proclus, 600 B.C. to A.D 500*, New York: Mentor Books, 1961, page 8.

[42] Ibid.

[43] Jung, C. G., *Memories, Dreams, Reflections*, New York: Vintage Books, 1989, page 318.

[44] Wellek, René, and Austin Warren, *Theory of Literature*, New York: Harcourt, Brace & World, Inc., 1956, page 207.

[45] Hansen, Ron, *Mariette in Ecstasy*, New York: HarperCollins Publishers, 1991, page 179.

[46] Steinbeck, John, *The Grapes of Wrath*, New York: Penguin Group, 1939, pages 580-1.

[47] Hemingway, Ernest, *A Farewell to Arms*, New York: Charles Scribner's Sons, 1929, page 3.

Endnotes

[48] Ibid, page 7.

[49] Fitzgerald, F. Scott, *The Great Gatsby*, New York: Charles Scribner's Sons, 1925, pages 3-4.

[50] Ibid, page 30.

[51] Lee, Chang-Rae, *Native Speaker*, New York: Riverhead Books, 1995, page 101.

[52] Ibid, page 346.

[53] Persig, Robert M., *Zen and the Art of Motorcycle Maintenance, An Inquiry into Values*, New York: Bantam Books, 1974, page 95.

[54] Flaubert, Gustave, *Madame Bovary*, tr. by Alan Russell, New York: Penguin Group, 1950, page 81.

[55] Scheid, John, and Jesper Svenbro, *The Craft of Zeus: Myths of Weaving and Fabric*, tr. by Carol Volk, Cambridge: Harvard University Press, 2001.

[56] These examples are from *Webster's New Collegiate Dictionary*, Springfield: G. & C. Merriam Company, 1979.

[57] Bolen, Jean Shinoda, M.D., *Gods in Everyman, A New Psychology of Men's Lives and Loves*, New York: Harper & Row, 1989, page 223.

[58] *Theophrastus: Characters, Herodas: Mimes, Sophron and Other Mime Fragments*, tr. and ed. by Jeffrey Rusten and I. C. Cunningham, Cambridge: Harvard University Press, LCL, 2002, pages 73 and 97.

[59] Salter, James, *Light Years*, San Francisco: North Point Press, 1982, page 8.

[60] Schroedinger, Erwin, *What is Life? With Mind and Matter and Autobiographical Sketches*, Cambridge: Cambridge University Press, 1992, page 122.

[61] Lilly, John C., *The Center of the Cyclone: Looking into Inner Space*, Oakland: Ronin Publishing, Inc., 1972. Entire book.

[62] Jung, Carl, *Collected Works*, Volume 4, Princeton: Princeton University Press, 1961, paragraph 728.

[63] Ibid, paragraph 405.

[64] Stein, Murray, *Jung's Map of the Soul*, Peru: Open Court, 1998, page 131.

[65] Ibid, page 132-3.

Endnotes

[66] Jung, C. G. and C. Kerenyi, *Essays on a Science of Mythology*, Princeton: Princeton University Press, 1959, page 173.

[67] Stein, Murray, *Jung's Map of the Soul*, Peru: Open Court, 1998, page 131.

[68] Hillman, James, *Archetypal Psychology, A Brief Account*, Dallas: Spring Publications, 1983, page 1.

[69] Ibid, page 3.

[70] From Thornton Wilder's Introduction (1955) to: Sophocles', *Oedipus The King*, translated by Francis Storr, Norwalk: The Easton Press, 1980, page 16.

[71] Kerenyi, C., *The Gods of the Greeks*, New York: Thames and Hudson, 1951, page 170.

[72] Jung, C. G., *The Spirit in Man, Art, and Literature*, Princeton: Princeton University Press, 1966, pages 73.

[73] Ibid, pages 81-2

[74] Burroway, Janet, *Writing Fiction, A Guide to Narrative Craft*, New York: Longman, 2000, pages 3-8.

[75] From *Facing the Gods*, ed. by James Hillman, Dallas: Spring Publications Inc., 1980, page 83.

[76] Jung, C. G., *The Spirit in Man, Art, and Literature*, tr. by R. F. C. Hull, Princeton: Princeton University Press, 1966, page 104.

[77] Dillard, Annie, *The Writing Life*, New York: Harper & Row, Publishers, 1989, page 16.

[78] Surmelian, Leon, *Techniques of Fiction Writing, Measure and Madness*, Garden City: Doubleday & Company, Inc., 1969, page 1.

[79] Joyce, James, *Ulysses*, New York: Random House, Inc., 1986, page 608.

[80] Ibid, 643-4.

[81] Hemingway, Ernest, *For Whom the Bell Tolls*, New York: Charles Scribner's Sons, 1940, page 3.

[82] Deleted.

[83] Delany, Samuel R., *Dhalgren*, New York: Bantam Books, 1975, page 1.

[84] *Webster's New Collegiate Dictionary*, Springfield: G. & C. Merriam Company,

Endnotes

1979.

[85] *Funk & Wagnalls Standard Dictionary*, Chicago: Encyclopaedia Britannica, Inc., 1965.

[86] *Webster's*, 1979.

[87] *Funk & Wagnalls*, 1965.

[88] Rilke, Rainer Maria, *Letters to a Young Poet*, tr. by M. D. Herter Norton, New York: W. W. Norton & Company, 1934, page 29.

Bibliography

1. Aristotle, *The Complete Works of Aristotle*, Princeton: Princeton University Press, 1984.
2. Blacker, Irwin R., *The Elements of Screenwriting*, New York: Collier Books, 1986.
3. Bolen, Jean Shinoda, M.D., *Gods in Everyman, A New Psychology of Men's Lives and Loves*, New York: Harper & Row, 1989.
4. Bradbury, Ray, *The Martian Chronicles*, New York: Bantam Books, 1958.
5. Burroway, Janet, *Writing Fiction, A Guide to Narrative Craft*, New York: Longman, 2000.
6. Colebrook, Claire, *Irony*, New York: Routledge, 2004.
7. de Santillana, Giorgio, *The Origins of Scientific thought, From Anaximander to Proclus, 600 B.C. to A.D 500*, New York: Mentor Books, 1961.
8. Dickens, Charles, *A Tale of Two Cities*, New York: Vintage Books, 1990.
9. Dillard, Annie, *The Writing Life*, New York: Harper & Row, Publishers, 1989.
10. Egri, Lajos, *The Art of Dramatic Writing*, New York: Simon & Schuster, Inc., 1960.
11. Eliot, George, *Adam Bede*, New York: Charles Schribner's Sons, 1917.
12. Euripides, *Euripides: Bacchae, Iphigenia at Aulis, Rhesus*, ed. and tr. by David Kovacs, Cambridge: Harvard University Press, LCL, 2002.
13. Field, Syd, *Screenplay, The Foundations of Screenwriting*, New York: Dell Publishing, 1994.
14. Fitzgerald, F. Scott, *The Great Gatsby*, New York: Charles Scribner's Sons, 1925.

Bibliography

15. Flaubert, Gustave, *Madame Bovary*, tr. by Alan Russell, New York: Penguin Group, 1950.

16. Forbes, R. J., *Studies in Ancient Technology*, Vol. VIII, Leiden: E. J. Brill, 1971.

17. Frank, Joseph, *Doestoevsky, The Miraculous Years, 1865-1871*, Princeton: Princeton University Press, 1995.

18. Furley, William D., *Studies in the Use of Fire in Ancient Greek Religion*, Salem: Ayer Company, Publishers, Inc., 1988.

19. James, Henry, *The Art of the Novel*, New York: Charles Schribner's Sons, 1934 (1907).

20. Hansen, Ron, *Mariette in Ecstasy*, New York: Edward Burlingame Books, 1991.

21. Hemingway, Ernest, *A Farewell to Arms*, New York: Charles Scribner's Sons, 1929.

22. ____, *For Whom the Bell Tolls*, New York: Charles Scribner's Sons, 1940.

23. Hesiod, *Theogony, Works and Days, Shield, tr.* by Apostolos N. Athanassakis, Baltimore: The Johns Hopkins University Press, 1983.

24. Hillman, James, *Archetypal Psychology, A Brief Account*, Dallas: Spring Publications, 1983.

25. ____, editor, *Facing the Gods*, Dallas: Spring Publications, 1980.

26. Homer, *The Iliad*, tr. by Robert Fitzgerald, Franklin Center: The Franklin Library, 1952.

27. ____, *The Iliad*, tr. by Martin Hammond, New York: Penguin Books, 1987.

28. ____, *The Odyssey*, tr. by Robert Fitzgerald, Franklin Center: The Franklin Library, 1978.

29. Joyce, James, *Ulysses*, New York: Random House, Inc., 1986.

30. Jung, Carl G, *The Archetypes and the Collective Unconscious*,

Princeton: Princeton University Press, 1959.

31. ____, *Collected Works*, Volume 4, Princeton: Princeton University Press, 1961.

32. ____ and C. Kerenyi, *Essays on a Science of Mythology*, Princeton: Princeton University Press, 1959.

33. ____, *Memories, Dreams, Reflections*, New York: Vintage Books, 1989.

34. ____, *The Spirit in Man, Art, and Literature*, Princeton: Princeton University Press, 1966.

35. Kerenyi, C., *The Gods of the Greeks*, New York: Thames and Hudson, 1951.

36. Kerenyi, Karl, *Hermes, Guide of Souls*, Dallas: Spring Publications, Inc., 1976.

37. Kundera, Milan, *The Art of the Novel*, New York: Harper & Row, Publishers, Inc., 1988.

38. Lee, Chang-Rae, *Native Speaker*, New York: Riverhead Books, 1995.

39. Lilly, John C., *The Center of the Cyclone: Looking into Inner Space*, Oakland: Ronin Publishing, Inc., 1972.

40. Mantel, Hilary, *Beyond Black*, New York: Henry Holt and Company LLC, 2004.

41. McInerney, Jay, *Bright Lights, Big City*. New York: Vintage Books, 1984.

42. Melville, Herman, *Moby Dick or, the Whale*, New York: Dell Publishing Co., Inc., 1959.

43. Moore, T. Sturge, *Art and Life*, London: Methuen, 1910.

44. Pirsig, Robert, *Zen and the Art of Motorcycle Maintenance, An Inquiry into Values*. New York: Bantam Books, 1974.

45. Rilke, Rainer Maria, *Letters to a Young Poet*, tr. by M. D. Herter Norton, New York: W. W. Norton & Company, 1934.

Bibliography

46. Salter, James, *Light Years*, San Francisco: North Point Press, 1982.

47. Scheid, John, and Jesper Svenbro, *The Craft of Zeus: Myths of Weaving and Fabric*, tr. by Carol Volk, Cambridge: Harvard University Press, 2001.

48. Schroedinger, Erwin, *What is Life? With Mind and Matter and Autobiographical Sketches*, Cambridge: Cambridge University Press, 1992.

49. Surmelian, Leon, *Techniques of Fiction Writing, Measure and Madness*, Garden City: Anchor Books, 1969.

50. Stein, Murray, *In Midlife*, Woodstock: Spring Publications 1983.

51. ___, *Jung's Map of the Soul*, Peru: Open Court, 1998.

52. Steinbeck, John, *The Grapes of Wrath*, New York: Penguin Group, 1939.

53. *Theophrastus: Characters, Herodas: Mimes, Sophron and Other Mime Fragments*, tr. and ed. by Jeffrey Rusten and I. C. Cunningham, Cambridge: Harvard University Press, LCL, 2002.

54. von Bothmer, Dietrich, *The Amasis Painter and His World, Vase-Painting in Sixth-Century B.C. Athens*, New York: Thames and Hudson ltd., and Malibu: The J. Paul Getty Museum, 1985.

55. Walker, Alice, *The Color Purple*, New York: Pocket Books, 1982.

56. Wellek, René, and Austin Warren, *Theory of Literature*, New York: Harcourt, Brace & World, Inc., 1956.

57. Whiteley, Opal, *The Singing Creek Where the Willows Grow, The Rediscovered Diary of Opal Whiteley*, presented by Benjamin Hoff, New York: Ticknor & fields, 1986.

Index

A

Achilles vi, 12, 78
Aeschylus xi
Aesop 88
agents 193, 195, 196, 197
Amazon.com 141, 198
American novel 23, 63, 72, 186
angel 162
anguish of choice 43, 45, 46, 56, 59, 78, 79, 133
anima 154, 155, 156, 157, 158, 161, 163
anima/us 154, 155, 156, 157, 158, 163
animus 154, 155, 158
antagonist 16, 17, 21, 23, 26, 31, 38, 39, 40, 41, 42, 46, 48, 56, 61, 127, 133
archetypal images 152, 153, 154, 156, 159
archetypal psychology xii, 49, 159
Ariadne 151
Aristotle 12, 41, 87, 209, 215
Art viii, 10, 125, 189, 209, 210, 212, 213, 215, 216, 217
Asklepios 162
Aspen Writers Conference 186
Association of Authors Representatives (AAR) 193
atmosphere 12, 60, 120
author/character relationship 35
authorial distance 73
author's glow 173

B

Bach, Richard 64, 79, 139, 166
backstory 74
Bates, Marilyn 48
beginning vii, viii, 16, 20, 21, 22, 23, 24, 25, 29, 43, 44, 57, 64, 65, 70, 74,
    78, 111, 114, 117, 119, 125, 126, 156, 164, 167, 176, 181

219

Index

Index

Index

evoking the senses 99

F

Faulkner, William 190
fictional world 11, 35, 37, 65, 67, 73, 80, 84, 95, 96, 97, 119, 122, 127, 128,
　　　130, 138, 147, 148, 163, 166, 180, 185
first chapter 111, 115, 116, 185, 195
first-person narration 53, 70, 94
first plot point 24, 27
First Plot Point 24, 25, 204
Fitzgerald, F. Scott 28, 29, 30, 49, 68, 116, 120, 122, 210, 212, 215, 216
flashback 74, 75
Flaubert, Gustave 36, 68, 126, 212, 216
Frank, Joseph 70, 71, 210, 216
Freud ix, x, xi, 148, 159, 167

G

good and evil 20, 30, 31
Grand Illusion 95
Greece x, 22, 47, 162
Groups as Characters 57

H

hallucinate 98, 147
Hansen, Ron 74, 117, 118, 210, 211, 216
heart of character 40
Hemingway, Ernest 100, 101, 102, 119, 120, 124, 184, 190, 211, 213, 216
Hephaestus vi, 12, 135
Hera 162
Hermes 162, 163, 164, 168, 170, 171, 217
hero 7, 39, 59, 60, 116
Herodotus 146
Hesiod xi, 85, 86, 211, 216
high concept 8
Hillman, James xi, 159, 213, 216

Index

Index

Index

Index

Index

storytelling vii, viii, x, xi, xii, 9, 18, 22, 23, 27, 31, 65, 73, 105, 106, 108,
    124, 143, 144, 157, 183
style 62, 63
subconscious 22, 98, 138, 160
subplot 57
suspense 78
Svenbro, Jesper 127, 212, 218
synopsis 21, 194, 196

T

taste 36, 95, 96, 97, 98, 99, 138, 145, 176
Teiresias 93
tension 17, 69, 73, 93, 115, 184
Thematic Character 56
theme 109
Theseus 7, 151
Tolkien, J. R. R. 57, 60, 69
total sensory deprivation 37, 96, 102, 146, 147, 185
touch 95, 96, 97, 98, 100, 101, 103, 117, 138, 145, 188, 202
tragic flaw 41
transcendence 157
transitions 125
Tyler, Anne 52

U

unconscious 75, 108, 150, 152, 153, 154, 155, 156, 157, 158, 159, 160, 161,
    162, 163, 164, 165, 171, 172, 174
University of Colorado 186

V

verbal irony 88
villain 39

W

Index